SINGER

SEWING REFERENCE LIBRARY®

Sewing for the Holidays

Cy DeCosse Incorporated
Minnetonka, Minnesota

Country scarecrow (above), page 114.

Learn to wrap presents creatively with fabric, using circular gift wraps, rolled gift wraps, or gift bags. All these styles are reversible and can be used again in future years. You can embellish the packages with wired ribbons or tassels you make yourself.

The Easter section features an old-fashioned stuffed rabbit and a basket decorated with ribbon. To set the table for Easter, make a tablecloth and coordinating napkins embellished with lace. You will even find ideas for a decorated Easter tree.

The final section contains projects for Halloween and Thanksgiving. Decorate for Halloween with stuffed pumpkins in two sizes, placing them on a table or mantel next to a cleverly made scarecrow. Also learn to make stiffened fabric ghosts and delight children with confetti placemats, perfect for a Halloween party. For Thanksgiving, make a fabric cornucopia. Fill it with colorful latex fruit or miniature pumpkins and Indian corn to make an interesting centerpiece. Whatever holiday you are sewing for, this book is sure to offer lots of ideas for holiday decorating.

Tassels (right), page 73.

Christmas

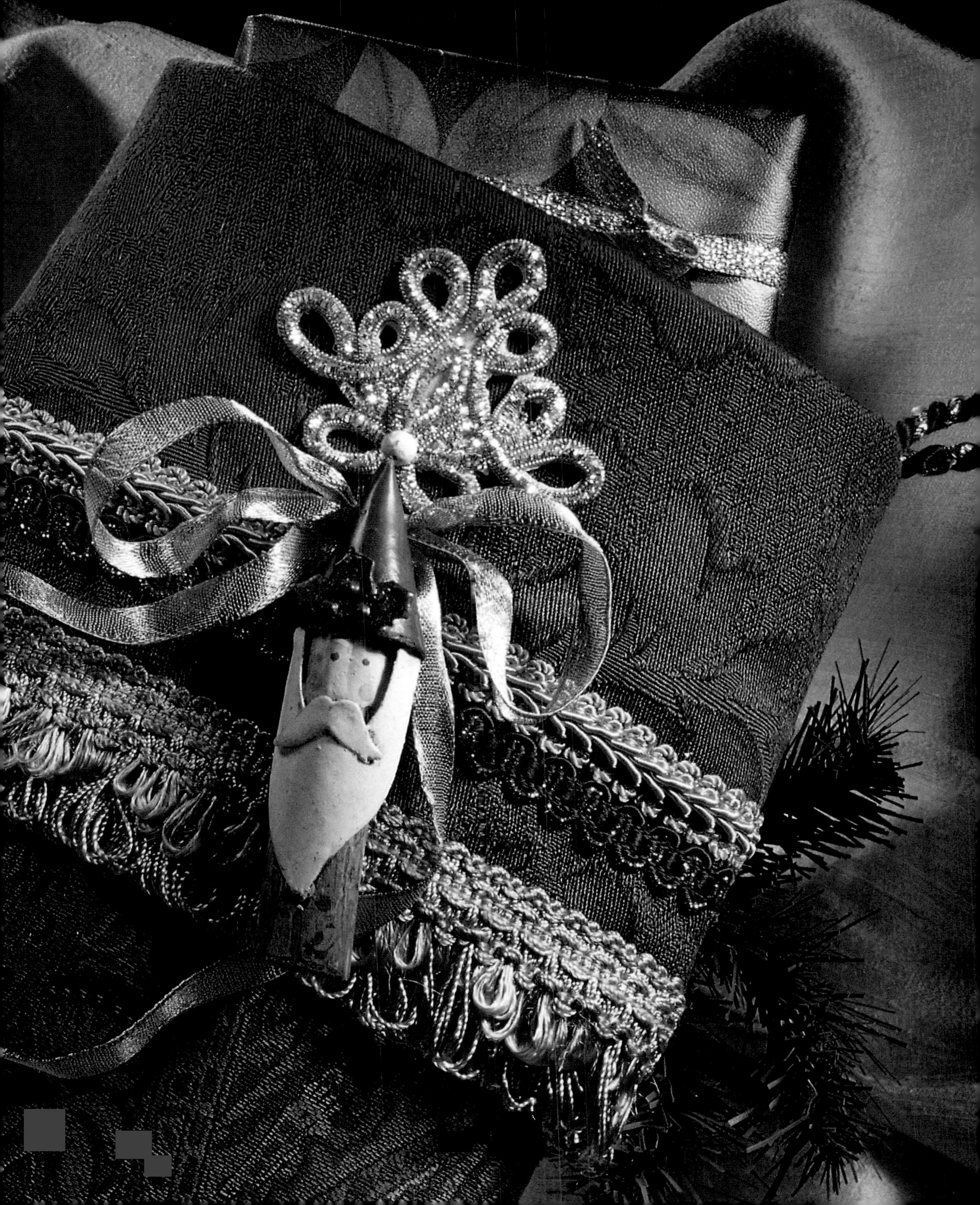

Lace Doily Ornaments

Lace doily ornaments, shaped as wreaths, semicircles, and baskets, give a Victorian look to a Christmas tree.

By using the ornaments, instead of bows, on packages, they become an extra keepsake gift.

Make the ornaments easily from Battenberg lace or cutwork doilies. Add ribbon hangers, and embellish the ornaments with trimmings such as dried or silk flowers or pearl strands.

YOU WILL NEED

For lace doily wreath or semicircle ornament:

Two 6" (15 cm) Battenberg or cutwork doilies, for lace wreath, or one for lace semicircle.

Polyester fiberfill.

9" (23 cm) length of ribbon or braid trim, for hanger.

Embellishments, such as dried or silk floral materials, pearl strands, and ribbon.

Hot glue gun and glue sticks, optional.

For lace doily basket ornament:

One 8" (20.5 cm) Battenberg or cutwork doily: one doily makes two ornaments.

9" (23 cm) length of ribbon or braid trim, for hanger.

Embellishments, such as dried or silk floral materials, optional.

Hot glue gun and glue sticks, optional.

How to Sew a Lace Doily Wreath Ornament

1) **Baste** ends of ribbon to wrong side of doily, about 1¼" (3.2 cm) from center. Mark 1" (2.5 cm) circle in center of one doily on wrong side. Pin the doilies right sides together.

2) **Stitch** around circle on marked line, using short stitch length. Trim away the fabric on the inside of circle ⅛" (3 mm) from stitching; turn right side out through center.

3) **Stitch** around doilies, along the inner edge of lace trim, or 1" (2.5 cm) from previous stitching; leave 2" (5 cm) opening.

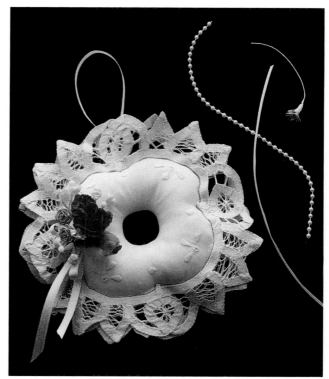

4) **Stuff** the wreath with polyester fiberfill; stitch opening closed by machine, using zipper foot. Secure embellishments with hot glue or by hand-stitching them in place.

How to Sew a Lace Doily Semicircle Ornament

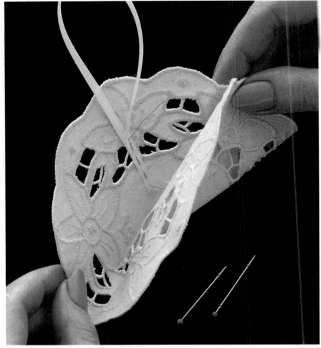

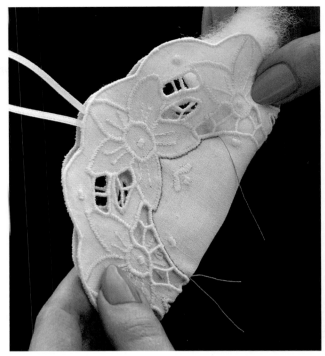

1) Baste ends of ribbon to wrong side of doily, about ¾" (2 cm) from center of doily. Fold doily in half.

2) Stitch around semicircle, along inner edge of lace, or 1" (2.5 cm) from outer edge, using short stitch length; leave 1" (2.5 cm) opening. Complete as in step 4, opposite.

How to Sew a Lace Doily Basket Ornament

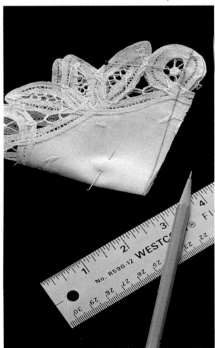

1) Cut doily in half. Fold one doily piece in half again, right sides together; mark point on raw edge at fold. Mark point on outer curved edge ½" (1.3 cm) from cut edge; draw line connecting points.

2) Cut on the marked line. Stitch ¼" (6 mm) from raw edge, using short stitch length. Turn right side out; press.

3) Stitch ribbon to each side of the basket; seam is at the center back. Secure any embellishments with hot glue or by hand-stitching in place.

Cookie-cutter Ornaments

Cookie cutters provide a variety of shapes to be used as patterns for tree ornaments. To make the patterns, simply trace around the cookie cutters and add ¼" (6 mm) seam allowances. Stitch the ornaments wrong sides together and leave the seams exposed for a homespun look.

Make the ornaments from cotton or cotton-blend fabrics. Add decorative details to the ornaments with fabric paints in fine-tip tubes. Hand-paint your own designs or follow the imprints of plastic or metal cookie cutters as a guide for painting the details.

For best results in painting, prewash the fabrics to remove sizing. Practice painting on a scrap of fabric before painting on the ornaments to perfect the painting techniques. To keep the paint flow even, tap the tip of the bottle gently on the table to eliminate air bubbles. Wipe the tip of the bottle often while painting, to prevent paint buildup. If the tip becomes clogged, squeeze the tube to force paint through the tip onto a sheet of paper or a paper towel. If necessary, remove the cap and unclog the tip with a toothpick or needle.

✂ Cutting Directions

Make the patterns as on page 16, step 1. For each ornament, cut two pieces from fabric, wrong sides together.

YOU WILL NEED

Scraps of cotton fabric in desired colors.
Polyester fiberfill.
9" (23 cm) length of ribbon or cording, for hanger.
Fabric paints in fine-tip tubes, for decorating ornaments.

How to Make a Cookie-cutter Ornament

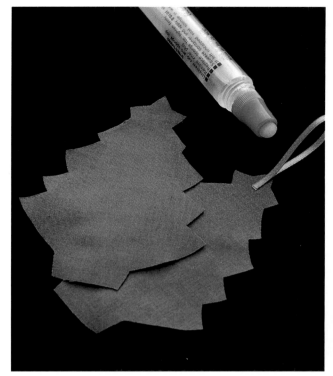

1) Transfer cookie-cutter design to paper by tracing around cookie cutter with a pencil; add ¼" (6 mm) seam allowances.

2) Cut fabric pieces for ornaments as on page 15. Fold ribbon in half to make hanger; glue-baste to top of ornament as shown.

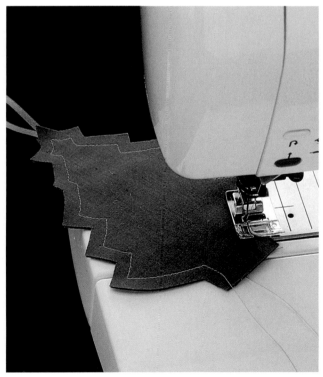

3) Place the fabric pieces *wrong* sides together; pin. Stitch ¼" (6 mm) from raw edges, using short stitch length; leave 1" (2.5 cm) opening for stuffing.

4) Stuff ornament with polyester fiberfill; use eraser end of a pencil to push stuffing into smaller areas.

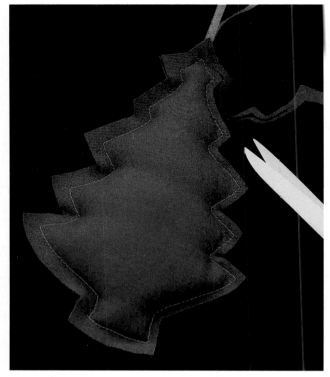

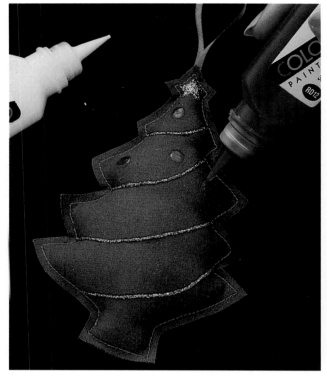

5) Stitch opening closed, using a zipper foot. Trim seam allowance to ⅛" (3 mm), taking care not to trim off hanger.

6) Add painted details to the ornaments as desired, using fabric paints.

Tips for Making Cookie-cutter Ornaments

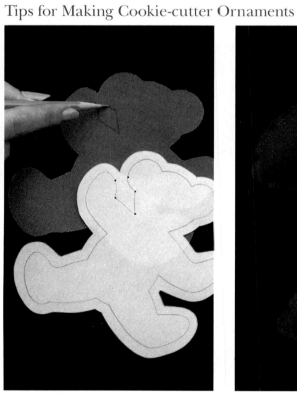

Mark stitching lines lightly with pencil or chalk when the seam allowances overlap.

Paint details on ornaments, using paint tube as a pencil; keep point on fabric while painting to get the finest line.

Trim around the ornament, using pinking shears, if desired, for a decorative edge finish.

Ornaments from Fabric Cutouts

Designs cut from some printed fabrics can be used to make two styles of tree ornaments: a basic cutout ornament and an appliquéd cutout ornament. Both styles are stitched and turned and have cutout designs on one or both sides.

Make basic cutout ornaments using a fabric cutout for the front of the ornament and a solid or coordinating fabric for the back. Or, for symmetrical designs, cut two motifs that are alike and use one for the front of

the ornament and one for the back. The shapes of the basic cutout ornaments follow the outline of the cutout designs.

The appliquéd cutout ornaments are cut to simple shapes like rectangles, circles, stars, and Christmas stockings, with the cutout designs used as appliqués. A cup, glass, or cookie cutter may be used as a template for the simple shapes. The cutout designs are fused to the ornaments before the ornaments are stuffed.

Cutout designs can easily be found in fabrics printed with Christmas motifs, but fabrics with floral, animal, or western motifs may also work well for both styles.

✂ Cutting Directions

For a basic cutout ornament, cut the design motif and the ornament back as on page 20, step 1. For an appliquéd cutout ornament, cut the ornament front and back to the desired shape, right sides together. The design motif is cut on page 21, step 3.

YOU WILL NEED

Scraps of printed fabric, for cutouts.

Scraps of solid or coordinating fabric.

9" (23 cm) length of ribbon or braid trim, for hanger.

Polyester fiberfill.

Paper-backed fusible web, for appliquéd cutout ornaments.

How to Sew a Basic Cutout Ornament

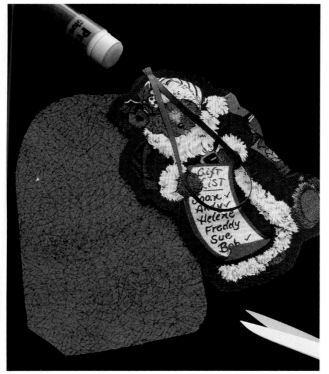

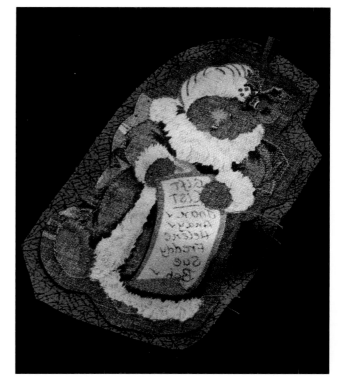

1) Cut design for ornament front from printed fabric, cutting ¼" (6 mm) outside the edge of design. Cut a piece of solid or coordinating fabric slightly larger than design, for ornament back. Baste ends of ribbon to upper edge on right side of design.

2) Pin front to back, right sides together. Stitch close to outer edge of design, about ¼" (6 mm) from raw edge, using short stitch length. Leave about 2" (5 cm) opening for turning.

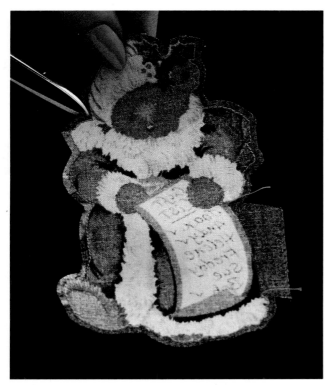

3) Trim close to stitching, clipping as necessary. Turn ornament right side out; press lightly.

4) Stuff ornament with polyester fiberfill. Hand-stitch opening closed.

How to Sew an Appliquéd Cutout Ornament

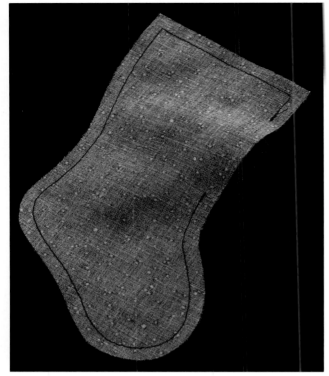

1) Baste ends of ribbon to the upper edge on right side of one ornament piece. Pin front to back, right sides together; stitch ¼" (6 mm) from raw edges, using short stitch length. Leave about 2" (5 cm) opening for turning.

2) Trim close to stitching, clipping as necessary. Turn ornament right side out; press. Apply paper-backed fusible web to wrong side of printed fabric, over the desired design, following manufacturer's directions.

3) Cut design from fabric. Remove the paper backing from fusible web, and fuse the design to ornament; allow to cool.

4) Stuff ornament with polyester fiberfill. Hand-stitch opening closed.

Quilt Ornaments

Decorate a tree with quilt ornaments that have an old-fashioned country appearance. These reversible ornaments feature a design motif, such as a Christmas tree or snowman, on the front and back, and, to resemble quilts, have binding on all sides.

The design motifs are fused to the blocks, using paper-backed fusible web. Complex designs are easily made by using different colors of fabric for the small details of the designs. Fine details can be added to the design with a fine-point permanent-ink marker.

Make patterns for design motifs by tracing designs from printed fabrics, wrapping paper, or cards. Look for simple design motifs, such as stockings, trees, or gingerbread men.

Use traditional cotton calicoes for the ornaments, or use seasonal red-and-green Christmas prints. Choose fabrics with washed-out colors to give the ornaments an antique or old-fashioned appearance. Hang the ornaments with a piece of twine to emphasize the country look.

22

✂ Cutting Directions

Cut two 3" × 4" (7.5 × 10 cm) rectangles each, from both the background fabric and polyester fleece. Cut one 2½" × 18" (6.5 × 46 cm) rectangle from the fabric for the binding.

Cut the design motifs from scraps of fabric as in steps 1 and 2, below.

YOU WILL NEED

Scraps of fabric, for design motifs, background, and binding.

Polyester fleece.

Paper-backed fusible web.

11" (28 cm) length of twine, for hanger.

Fine-point permanent-ink marker.

How to Sew a Quilt Ornament

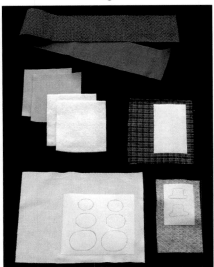

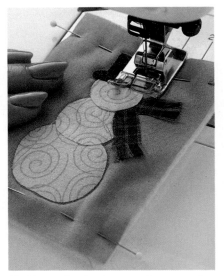

1) Cut the fabric rectangles from background fabric and fleece, as above. Apply paper-backed fusible web to scraps of fabric for design motifs, following manufacturer's directions. Transfer design motifs onto paper side of fusible web.

2) Cut design motifs from paper-backed fabric; remove paper backing. Fuse motifs to background rectangles for ornament front and back.

3) Place the background rectangle for front over fleece; pin. Quilt the design motif by stitching around outer edges of the design. Repeat for back.

4) Pin the quilted rectangles wrong sides together. Make binding and apply to edges of ornament as on page 49, steps 7 to 9. Tie a knot ½" (1.3 cm) from each end of twine. Hand-stitch knotted ends to the upper corners of the ornament.

5) Add fine details to the ornament with a fine-point permanent-ink marker.

Heart
Ornaments

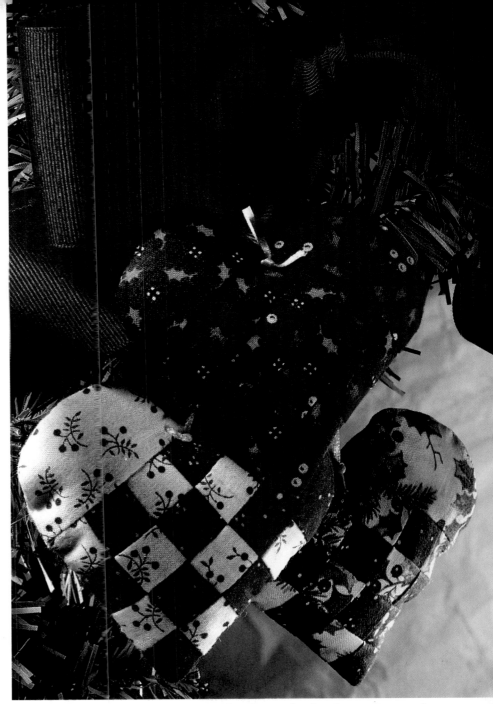

Heart ornaments in two styles complement each other on the Christmas tree. The checkerboard effect is dominant in both the no-sew heart basket and the stitched heart. In the heart basket, the checkerboard pattern is achieved by weaving fabric strips together. In the stitched heart, the checkerboard effect is created by piecing fabric strips together.

For the outside of the heart basket and for the stitched heart, use two coordinating Christmas prints or two solid-color fabrics. Select a fabric in a coordinating color to line the inside of the heart basket. For variety, make several heart ornaments in different fabrics, both solid and printed. Use braid trim or ribbon for the hangers.

✂ Cutting Directions

For a heart basket ornament, cut the fabric pieces as on page 26, steps 1 to 3.

For a stitched heart ornament, cut a 1" (2.5 cm) strip across the width of each fabric, then cut the strips in half to make two 1" (2.5 cm) strips of each fabric. Also cut two 1½" × 2½" (3.8 × 6.5 cm) rectangles from each fabric.

Stitched heart ornaments are clustered to form a focal point on the wreath above. A heart basket filled with candy hangs from the tree opposite.

YOU WILL NEED

For heart basket ornament:
⅛ yd. (0.15 m) each of two coordinating fabrics, in cotton or cotton blends.
⅛ yd. (0.15 m) fabric, in cotton or cotton blend, for lining.
⅝ yd. (0.6 m) narrow braid trim or ribbon, for hanger and bow.
Paper-backed fusible web.
Thick white craft glue.

For stitched heart ornament:
⅛ yd. (0.15 m) each of two coordinating fabrics, in cotton or cotton blends.
9" (23 cm) length of ribbon or braid trim, for hanger.
Polyester fiberfill.

How to Make a Heart Basket Ornament

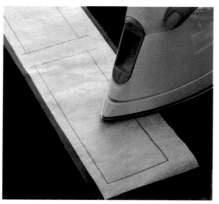

1) **Trace** partial template for heart basket ornament (opposite) onto paper, with dotted line of template on fold of paper. Cut on solid line to make full-size template.

2) **Draw** two 2½" × 7½" (6.5 × 19.3 cm) rectangles on paper side of paper-backed fusible web. Apply fusible web to lining, following the manufacturer's directions. Cut out rectangles.

3) **Remove** paper backing, and fuse lining pieces to contrasting outer fabrics. Trim outer fabric to match lining pieces.

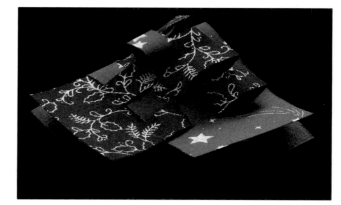

4) **Fold** each rectangle in half crosswise; press. Mark points along fold at ⅝" (1.5 cm) intervals, using chalk. Mark chalk line parallel to, and 2½" (6.5 cm) from, the fold. Clip fabric from the marked points at fold to marked chalk line.

5) **Weave** red and green strips together by alternately inserting loops through each other.

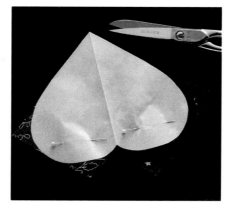

6) **Continue** weaving red and green strips together as shown.

7) **Place** heart template over basket, aligning point of basket with point of heart; pin. Trim away the excess fabric around curve of heart.

8) **Secure** a 9" (23 cm) length of ribbon for handle on each side of heart basket between fabric strips, using glue. Tie two bows from the remaining ribbon; glue bows to each side of basket.

How to Make a Stitched Heart Ornament

1) **Trace** partial template for stitched heart ornament onto paper, with dotted line of template on fold of paper. Cut on solid line to make full-size template.

2) **Stitch** four fabric strips together lengthwise, using ¼" (6 mm) seams and alternating colors. Press seam allowances in one direction.

3) **Cut** eight 1" (2.5 cm) strips across pieced strip. Stitch pieced strips together, using ¼" (6 mm) seams, to make two checkerboard units, each 2½" (6.5 cm) square.

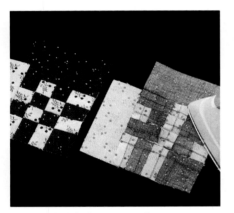

4) **Stitch** fabric rectangles to two adjacent sides of the checkerboard units, in ¼" (6 mm) seams. Press seam allowances toward rectangles. Pin units right sides together.

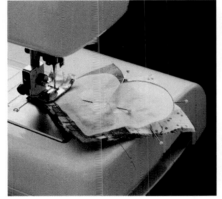

5) **Pin** template to checkerboard units, ¼" (6 mm) from raw edges of checkerboard. Stitch around the template, using short stitches; leave 1½" (3.8 cm) opening on one side.

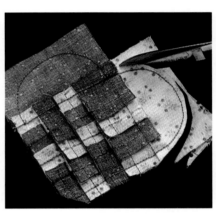

6) **Trim** close to point and curves; clip inner corner. Turn right side out; press.

7) **Stuff** heart lightly with polyester fiberfill. Hand-stitch the opening closed. Tie knots in both ends of the ribbon hanger; hand-stitch one end to each side of heart at top.

Templates for Heart Ornaments

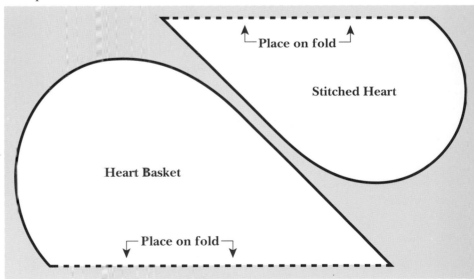

Place on fold

Stitched Heart

Heart Basket

Place on fold

Tree Skirts

Tree skirts add the finishing touch to a decorated Christmas tree. Unlined tree skirts are simple to make and provide an elegant look in both square and round styles. The tree skirts can lie flat around the base of the tree, or they can be draped to create folds in the fabric. For more folds, select fabrics that are 60" (152.5 cm) wide.

Embellishing the tree skirts around the edges with decorative trims eliminates the need for hemming. On a square tree skirt, use gimp trim and add tassels (page 73) at the corners. On a round tree skirt, stitch gimp trim to the back opening and the inner circle only, and stitch fringe trim to the outer edge.

✂ Cutting Directions

For either a square or round tree skirt, cut a 45" (115 cm) or 60" (152.5 cm) square from fabric. The round tree skirt will be trimmed to the exact size and shape on page 31, step 1.

YOU WILL NEED

1¼ yd. fabric (1.15 m), 45" (115 cm) wide, for a 45" (115 cm) tree skirt or 1⅔ yd. (1.58 m) fabric, 60" (152.5 cm) wide, for a 60" (152.5 cm) tree skirt.

6⅝ yd. (6.1 m) gimp, for a 45" (115 cm) square tree skirt; or 9 yd. (8.25 m) for a 60" (152.5 cm) square tree skirt.

1⅝ yd. (1.5 m) gimp and 3⅞ yd. (3.55 m) fringe, for a 45" (115 cm) round tree skirt, or 2⅛ yd. (1.95 m) gimp and 5⅝ yd. (5.15 m) fringe, for a 60" (152.5 cm) round tree skirt.

Four tassels, for square tree skirt.

Liquid fray preventer.

Tree skirts can be made in two styles. The round tree skirt above features fringe trim around the outer edge. The square tree skirt opposite is embellished with gimp trim and tassels.

How to Sew a Square Tree Skirt

1) **Fold** the fabric in half lengthwise, then crosswise. Mark an arc, measuring 1¾" (4.5 cm) from folded center of fabric. Cut on marked line.

2) **Cut** along one folded edge; this will be the center back of tree skirt.

3) **Pin** gimp trim to tree skirt, *wrong* sides together, so edge of trim overlaps by a scant ⅜" (1 cm); pivot trim at corners, and ease trim around inner circle. Apply liquid fray preventer to cut ends of gimp.

4) **Stitch** close to the inner edge of gimp, starting ⅜" (1 cm) from end; pivot at corners, and continue stitching to starting point.

5) **Fold** to right side; fold in excess fullness at corners, making a small tuck as shown. Press gimp.

6) **Position** tassels at corners of tree skirt, concealing cord of tassel under trim; secure. Fold under end of gimp trim at end; trim away excess.

7) Stitch close to inner edge of gimp. Pivot at corner, and stitch diagonally across gimp to hold tuck; stop with needle down at outer corner. (Presser foot was removed to show detail.)

8) Pivot, and stitch back across gimp to inner corner. Pivot, and continue stitching around tree skirt.

How to Sew a Round Tree Skirt

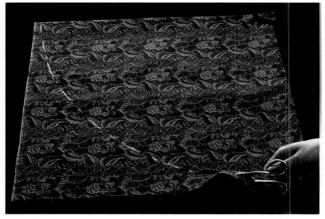

1) Fold fabric and mark arc as in step 1, opposite. Using a straightedge and pencil, mark an arc on fabric one-half the desired diameter of tree skirt from folded center of fabric. Cut on marked line through all layers.

2) Continue as in step 2, opposite. Apply gimp trim to tree skirt along center back and inner circle, as in steps 3 and 4, opposite, stitching gimp to ends.

3) Fold gimp to right side; press. Stitch close to the inner edge of gimp.

4) Finish outer edge of tree skirt. Stitch fringe trim to tree skirt ½" (1.3 cm) from outer edge; extend fringe ¼" (6 mm) beyond ends at center back. Turn ends of fringe to wrong side; hand-stitch in place.

Victorian Stockings

Trim a mantel with one-of-a-kind Victorian Christmas stockings made from elegant fabrics, ornate trims, and handmade tassels. Choose embellishments like lace motifs, ribbons, rhinestones, or antique jewelry. Or weave ribbons over the entire stocking front.

Select fabrics like velvets, moirés, brocades, and tapestries, using matching or contrasting fabric for the stocking cuff. For the woven-ribbon stocking, also select satin, velvet, or organza ribbon, combining several types of ribbon in varying widths, if desired. To add body, pad the stockings with polyester fleece or low-loft quilt batting.

✄ Cutting Directions

Make the full-size pattern as on page 35. Place fabric right sides together, and cut two stocking pieces from the outer fabric and two from lining. Also cut two stocking pieces from the fleece or batting. For the stocking cuff, cut one 6" × 15¾" (15 × 40 cm) rectangle each from outer fabric, interfacing, and lining. The ribbons for the woven-ribbon stocking are cut during construction.

YOU WILL NEED

⅝ **yd. (0.6 m) fabric,** for stocking.

⅝ **yd. (0.6 m) fabric,** for lining.

⅝ **yd. (0.6 m) polyester fleece** or low-loft quilt batting.

¼ **yd. (0.25 m) fabric,** for contrasting cuff, if desired.

¼ **yd. (0.25 m) fusible interfacing,** for cuff.

4" **(10 cm) ribbon or cording,** for hanger.

Lace motifs, ribbons, jewelry, or rhinestones, for embellishments.

Assorted ribbons, for woven ribbon stocking; yardages vary.

Materials for optional tassel, listed on page 73.

Victorian stockings can be decorated with trims such as ribbon, gimp, and fringe. A combination of ribbons, including textured and printed ribbons, creates the woven-ribbon overlay for the stocking above. An emblem, a lace motif, and a piece of jewelry add to the embellished stockings opposite. Handmade tassels (page 73) add the finishing touch.

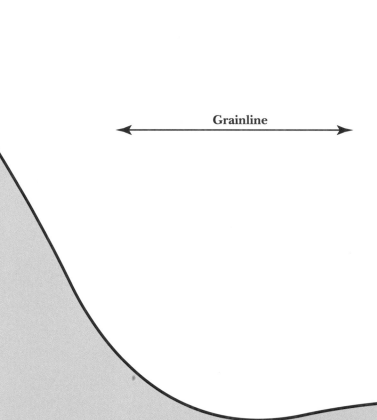

Stocking
Add ¹/₂" (1.3 cm) seam allowance

Grainline

How to Make a Full-size Pattern for a Victorian Stocking

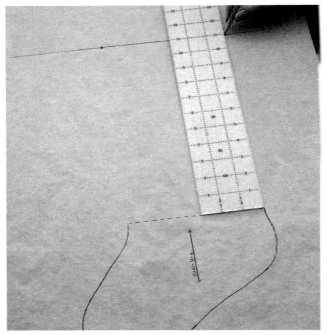

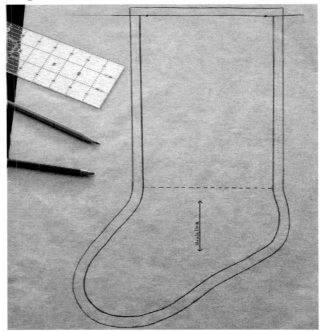

1) Trace partial pattern piece (opposite) onto tissue paper. Draw a line parallel to and 11" (28 cm) above dotted line to mark the upper edge of stocking. Align quilter's ruler to dotted line at side; mark a point on line for upper edge. Repeat for other side.

2) Measure out ⅜" (1 cm) from marked points; mark. Connect outer points at upper edge to sides at ends of dotted line. Add ½" (1.3 cm) seam allowances to make full-size stocking pattern.

How to Sew an Embellished Victorian Stocking

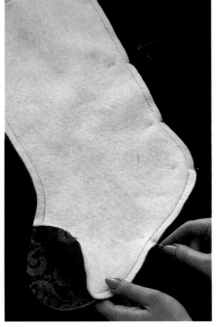

1) Cut stocking and cuff pieces as on page 33. Apply interfacing to the wrong side of the cuff, following the manufacturer's directions.

2) Plan placement of ribbon and other embellishments on cuff; pin or glue-baste in place. Stitch close to edges of trims.

3) Baste fleece or batting to wrong sides of stocking pieces. Pin stocking pieces right sides together.

(Continued on next page)

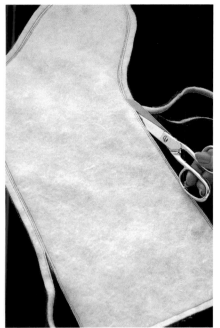

4) Stitch ½" (1.3 cm) seam around stocking, leaving top open. Stitch again next to first row of stitching, within seam allowance. Trim close to stitches. Turn stocking right side out; press lightly.

5) Fold cuff in half crosswise, right sides together. Stitch ½" (1.3 cm) seam; press seam open. Repeat for cuff lining.

6) Pin cuff to cuff lining on lower edge, right sides together, matching the seams. Stitch ½" (1.3 cm) seam around cuff; trim. Press seam toward lining: understitch as shown.

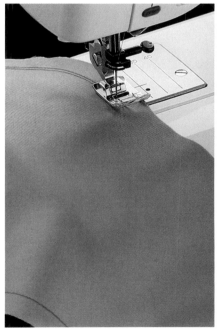

7) Turn cuff lining to inside; press. Baste cuff and cuff lining together at upper edge. Pin cuff to stocking, right sides up; baste at upper edge.

8) Make tassel, if desired (page 73). Fold ribbon or cording in half for hanger. At back seam, baste hanger and tassel to upper edge on right side of stocking.

9) Pin the lining pieces right sides together. Stitch ½" (1.3 cm) seam around lining, leaving the top open and bottom unstitched for 4" to 6" (10 to 15 cm); stitch again next to first row of stitching, within seam allowance. Trim close to stitches.

10) **Place** the outer stocking inside lining, right sides together. Pin and stitch around upper edges. Turn right side out through opening in lining.

11) **Stitch** opening closed. Insert lining into stocking; lightly press upper edge. Hand-stitch lace, jewelry, or other items to stocking, if desired, taking care not to catch lining.

How to Sew a Woven-ribbon Victorian Stocking

1) **Cut** stocking and cuff pieces as on page 33. Apply interfacing to the wrong side of the cuff, following manufacturer's directions. Plan placement of ribbon trims, and cut vertical ribbon trims to the desired lengths.

2) **Place** vertical ribbon lengths on stocking front; secure short ends to seam allowance at upper edge, using glue stick. Trims may be spaced slightly apart, if necessary.

3) **Weave** horizontal trims one row at a time; cut to length. Secure ends of ribbon with glue stick. Complete stocking as on pages 35 to 37, steps 2 to 11.

Pieced Stockings with Appliqués

Brightly colored pieced stockings, with simple appliqué designs, are especially appealing to children. These large stockings made from wool melton or felt are easy to sew. For more body, the felt stocking has an additional layer of felt fused to the front, cuff, and hanger pieces.

Find inspiration for the simple appliqué designs in a children's coloring book, or trace around a cookie cutter. A basic appliqué pattern for a snowflake can be made by folding a 5" (12.5 cm) circle of paper into quarters and making notches along the edges. Straight stitching around the appliqués holds them in place. The cuff and hanger of the stocking are edged with a blanket stitch.

✂ Cutting Directions

For a wool melton stocking, make the full-size pattern below. Cut one stocking back from fabric, with the right side of the fabric facing down. Cut fabric scraps into a variety of shapes for the pieced stocking front. Cut the stocking front from the pieced fabric section, right side up, after completing step 1 on page 40. Cut the desired appliqué designs from scraps of fabric. Cut one 6½" × 20" (16.3 × 51 cm) rectangle for the stocking cuff and one 1" × 8" (2.5 × 20.5 cm) rectangle for the stocking hanger.

For a felt stocking, make the full-size pattern below. Cut two stocking pieces, right sides together, from felt and one piece from fusible web. Cut felt scraps into a variety of shapes for the pieced stocking front. Cut two 6½" × 20" (16.3 × 51 cm) rectangles from felt and one from fusible web for the stocking cuff, and two 1" × 8" (2.5 × 20.5 cm) rectangles from felt and one from fusible web for the stocking hanger.

YOU WILL NEED

¾ yd. (0.7 m) wool melton, for stocking back; or **¾** yd. (0.7 m) felt, for stocking back and front underlining.

¼ yd. (0.25 m) wool melton or felt, for contrasting cuff.

1¼ yd. (1.15 m) lightweight fusible web, for felt stocking.

Scraps of wool melton or felt, for stocking front, appliqués, and stocking hanger.

Tear-away stabilizer, for wool melton stocking.

Pearl cotton or rayon thread, for blanket-stitch edging.

How to Make a Full-size Pattern for a Pieced Stocking with Appliqués

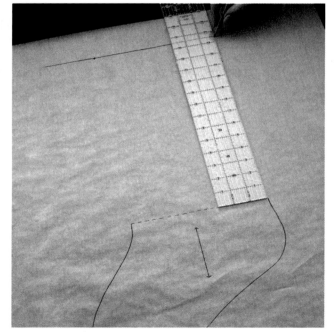

1) Enlarge partial pattern piece (page 34) by about 130 percent on a photocopy machine. Trace enlarged partial pattern onto tissue paper. Draw a line parallel to, and 13½" (34.3 cm) above, dotted line to mark upper edge of stocking. Align quilter's ruler to dotted line at side; mark point on line for upper edge. Repeat for other side.

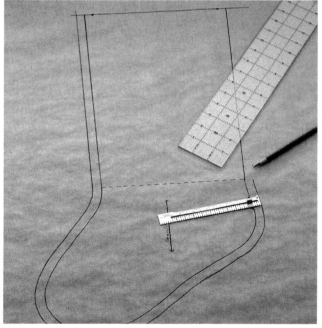

2) Measure out ½" (1.3 cm) from marked points; mark. Connect outer points at upper edge to sides at ends of dotted line. Add ½" (1.3 cm) seam allowances to make full-size stocking pattern.

How to Make a Pieced Stocking with Appliqués from Wool Melton

1) **Butt** the edges of fabric scraps for stocking front; place tear-away stabilizer under the scraps. Zigzag scraps together, using wide, closely spaced zigzag stitches. Remove the stabilizer. Cut stocking front as on page 38.

2) **Glue-baste** or pin appliqués to the stocking front; straight-stitch ⅛" (3 mm) from all edges of appliqués.

3) **Pin** stocking front to stocking back, right sides together. Stitch ½" (1.3 cm) seam, leaving top open. Stitch again next to first row of stitching, within seam allowances. Trim close to stitches. Turn stocking right side out; press lightly.

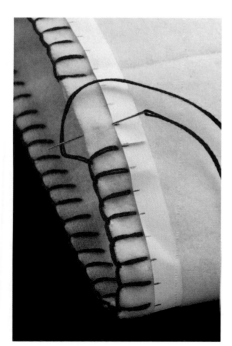

4) **Fold** cuff in half crosswise, right sides together. Stitch ½" (1.3 cm) seam. Stitch along the lower edge of cuff and long edges of hanger, using blanket stitch, opposite. Tape marked at ⅜" (1 cm) intervals may be used as a guide for stitching.

5) **Fold** the stocking hanger in half, wrong sides together. At back seam, baste stocking hanger to upper edge of stocking on the wrong side.

6) **Place** the right side of cuff on wrong side of stocking, matching back seams; pin along upper edge. Stitch ½" (1.3 cm) seam. Turn cuff to right side; press lightly.

How to Make a Pieced Stocking with Appliqués from Felt

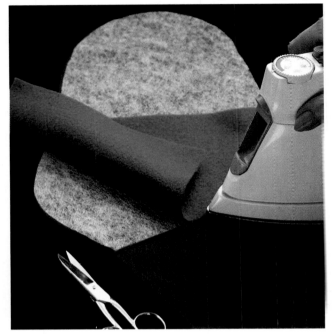

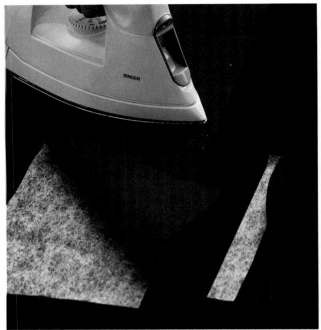

1) Cut stocking pieces as on page 38. Butt edges of felt scraps, and fuse to stocking front, using fusible web; follow manufacturer's directions for fusing. Zigzag over butted edges, using wide, closely spaced zigzag stitches. Trim felt scraps to match outline of stocking.

2) Fuse the cuff pieces and hanger pieces together, using fusible web. Complete stocking as in steps 2 to 6, opposite.

How to Blanket-stitch

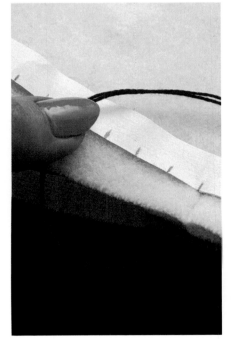

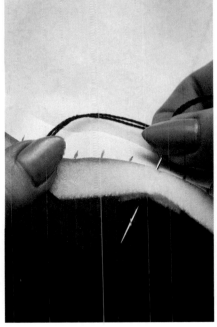

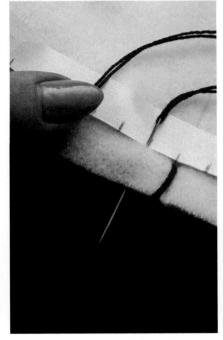

1) Take two short backstitches at lower edge of fabric, within seam allowance, to secure the thread. Form a loop at edge of fabric by bringing thread to left and then right as shown; hold loop with left thumb.

2) Insert needle to underside ½" (1.3 cm) from edge of fabric, then through loop as shown. Pull needle through fabric; release thumb from loop, then pull stitch tight.

3) Make second stitch ⅜" (1 cm) from first stitch as in steps 1 and 2; work stitches from right to left. Tape marked at ⅜" (1 cm) intervals may be used as a guide for stitching.

Trimmed Table Linens

Dress up a holiday table with elegantly trimmed placemats and napkins made from decorator fabrics. The unique shape of the placemat adds to the festive look. The instructions for the placemat can be varied to make a table runner, below.

For the placemats or table runner, choose a fabric that has body, such as brocade or tapestry. For the napkins, a lighter-weight fabric may be used.

Braid trim is used to edge both the placemats and napkins, eliminating the need for hemming. Wider trims can be created by stitching two rows of braid trim together. Vary the trims on the placemat and napkin to create interesting table settings. Add a purchased tassel to the placemat, or make your own as on page 73.

Elegant napkin rings complement the lavish table linens. They are made from cording and are embellished with decorative buttons or rhinestones.

Care for the table linens following the recommended method for the fabric and trim. Many decorator fabrics and trims require dry cleaning, but some may be washed by machine on gentle cycle, or by hand.

✂ Cutting Directions

For each placemat, cut one 20½" (52.3 cm) square from fabric. For each napkin, cut one 18" (46 cm) square from fabric. For each napkin ring, cut one length of cording, 1 yd. (0.95 m) long.

YOU WILL NEED

For four placemats:
1¼ yd. (1.15 m) fabric, at least 45" (115 cm) wide.
8 yd. (7.35 m) braid, such as gimp trim, for a single row of trim; or 16 yd. (14.72 m) braid, for a double row.
Four tassels.

For four napkins:
1⅛ yd. (1.05 m) fabric.
9 yd. (8.25 m) braid, such as gimp trim.

For four napkin rings:
4 yd. (3.7 m) cording.
Four decorative buttons or rhinestones.
Liquid fray preventer.
3" × 5" (7.5 × 12.5 cm) index card.

Table runner with tassels at the ends is a simple variation of the placemat. The length of the runner is equal to the length of the table, plus 7½" (19.3 cm) at each end for the drop.

How to Sew Trimmed Placemats and Napkins

Placemats. 1) Cut fabric square as on page 43. Mark point at center on the lower edge of fabric square. Mark points on sides 7½" (19.3 cm) from the lower edge. Draw lines connecting point at lower edge to side points. Cut along marked lines.

2) Pin gimp trim to *wrong* side of placemat, so edge of trim overlaps placemat by a scant ⅜" (1 cm); begin ¼" (6 mm) from point at lower edge. Pivot trim at corners, and apply liquid fray preventer to the cut ends of gimp.

3) Complete as on pages 30 and 31, steps 4 to 8, except in step 4, begin stitching at end of gimp.

Napkins. Complete napkin as on pages 30 and 31, steps 3 to 8; omit reference to inner circle in step 3 and tassels in step 6.

How to Make Trimmed Napkin Rings

1) Wrap cording around index card as shown, so three rows of cording are on the underside of the card and four rows are on top.

2) Wrap the end on the left over and under the remaining three rows of cording on top of the card, and bring end up.

3) Wrap end on right side over and under the three remaining rows of cording on top of card, and bring end up at right.

4) Wrap ends over top; remove card. Wrap ends to underside; secure ends together with hand stitches.

5) Trim excess cording. Prevent ends from raveling with liquid fray preventer. Stitch a decorative button or rhinestone to top of napkin ring.

Pine Trees Placemats & Table Runners

Quilted holiday placemats and a table runner are pieced in a Pine Trees design made from squares and right triangles. The right triangles are quickly and easily cut from fabric strips with the Easy Angle™ cutting tool designed for quilters. If you are not using an Easy Angle cutting tool, cut diagonally across 3⅜" (8.5 cm) fabric squares to make the right triangles.

A table runner can be made to fit any size table. The length of the runner is determined by the number of Pine Trees blocks that are stitched together. The directions that follow are for a runner of four blocks.

The quilt blocks can be constructed from either two or three fabric colors. In the projects shown here, two fabrics are used for the placemats, while the table runner has three fabrics for more variety.

✂ **Cutting Directions** (for one two-color placemat)
From Fabric A, cut four 2½" (6.5 cm) strips across the width of the fabric, to be used for the trees and the binding. From Fabric B, cut three 2½" (6.5 cm) strips across the width of the fabric, to be used for the trees and the background. As shown on page 48, steps 1 and 2, cut 30 triangles from the strips of Fabric A; cut 30 triangles and 18 squares from the strips of Fabric B.

Cut one 13" × 17" (33 × 43 cm) rectangle from the backing fabric and one from batting or fleece.

✂ **Cutting Directions** (for a three-color table runner)
From Fabric A, cut six 2½" (6.5 cm) strips across the width of the fabric, to be used for the trees. From Fabric B, cut four 2½" (6.5 cm) strips across the width of the fabric, to be used for the trees. From Fabric C, cut twelve 2½" (6.5 cm) strips across the width of the fabric, to be used for the background and the binding. As shown on page 48, steps 1 and 2, cut 30 triangles for each tree block from the strips of Fabric A and 18 triangles from the strips of Fabric B; cut 12 triangles and 18 squares for each tree block from the strips of Fabric C.

Cut one 13" × 66" (33 × 168 cm) rectangle from the backing fabric and one from batting or fleece; piece the backing fabric as necessary.

YOU WILL NEED

For four two-color placemats:
1⅓ yd. (1.27 m) Fabric A, for trees and binding.
1 yd. (0.95 m) Fabric B, for trees and background.
⅞ yd. (0.8 m) backing fabric.
1 yd. (0.95 m) low-loft quilt batting or polyester fleece.
Easy Angle cutting tool.

For one three-color table runner:
⅔ yd. (0.63 m) Fabric A, for trees.
½ yd. (0.5 m) Fabric B, for trees.
1⅛ yd. (1.05 m) Fabric C, for background and binding.
⅞ yd. (0.8 m) backing fabric.
2 yd. (1.85 m) low-loft quilt batting or polyester fleece.
Easy Angle cutting tool.

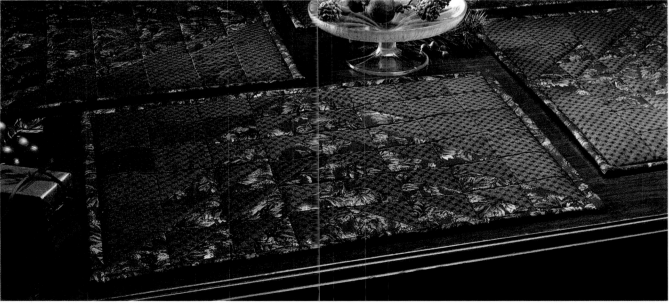

Quilted Pine Trees blocks are used to make the table runner and placemats above. Two fabrics are used for the placemats. The third fabric in the table runner gives a dominant Pine Trees effect from both sides.

1) Align Easy Angle™ cutting tool with fabric strip at marking for 2½" (6.5 cm) right triangle; cut along diagonal edge of tool.

2) Flip tool over, keeping diagonal edge of tool along diagonal cut of fabric. Align cutting tool with edge of fabric strip at marking for 2½" (6.5 cm) right triangle; cut along straight edge of tool. Continue to cut necessary number of triangles (page 46).

3) Stitch one triangle from Fabric A to one triangle from Fabric B, right sides together, along the long edge, in ¼" (6 mm) seam. Continue piecing triangles until 30 triangle-squares have been completed. Press seams toward tree fabric; trim off points.

4) Stitch background squares and triangle-squares together to make rows, as shown.

5) Stitch rows together, turning seams in opposite directions to reduce bulk. Press seams toward top of tree.

6) Layer backing, batting, and tree block; pin. Quilt tree by stitching over seamlines of tree, stitching in the well of the seam; stitch with hands positioned on either side of presser foot, holding fabric taut.

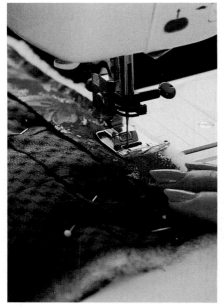

7) Press the binding strip in half lengthwise, wrong sides together. Pin binding strip to right side of the placemat on one long edge, matching raw edges. Stitch 1/4" (6 mm) from raw edges.

8) Wrap the binding strip snugly around edge of placemat, covering stitching line on back of placemat; pin. Stitch in the ditch on the right side of the placemat, catching the binding on back side.

9) Stitch the binding strip on the remaining long edge as in steps 7 and 8. Stitch binding strips on the short edges as in step 7; leave ends of binding extending 1/2" (1.3 cm) beyond the finished edges; secure binding as in step 8, folding ends over finished edges.

How to Sew a Pine Trees Table Runner

1) Follow steps 1 to 4, opposite. In step 3, stitch 18 triangle-squares, joining Fabrics A and B, and 12 triangle-squares, joining Fabrics A and C. Stitch the squares from Fabric C and triangle-squares together to make rows as shown.

2) Complete the block as in step 5, opposite. Make three additional blocks. Stitch the blocks, right sides together, along short edges, in 1/4" (6 mm) seams; press. Layer backing, batting, and runner top; pin.

3) Quilt trees as in step 6, opposite. Stitch in the ditch between the tree blocks. Trim batting and backing to match runner top, if necessary. Piece binding strips together on the bias as necessary. Bind edges of runner as in steps 7 to 9.

49

Noel Banners

Decorate a door or wall with a festive Noel banner that gives the look of stained glass. Although this banner looks very intricate, it is simple to make and involves very little piecing. The stained-glass effect is achieved by stitching strips of bias tape over the edges of fabric blocks and letters to conceal the raw edges. Hang the banner decoratively from a rod or dowel, using the tabs along the upper edge.

✂ Cutting Directions

The measurements for the following banner pieces include ¼" (6 mm) seam allowances:

For the background, cut four 7½" (19.3 cm) squares from Fabric A.

For the letters, enlarge the diagram, as on page 52, step 1. Cut one of each letter from Fabric B, as on page 52, step 2.

For the sashing, cut five 1½" × 7½" (3.8 × 19.3 cm) strips and two 1½" × 33½" (3.8 × 85.3 cm) strips from Fabric C.

For the inner border strips, cut two 3½" × 33½" (9 × 85.3 cm) rectangles and two 3½" × 15½" (9 × 39.3 cm) rectangles from Fabric D. For the stained-glass squares on the inner border strips, cut thirty-two 2⅛" (5.3 cm) squares from scraps of fabric.

For the outer border strips, cut two 3½" × 39½" (9 × 100.3 cm) rectangles and two 3½" × 21½" (9 × 54.8 cm) rectangles from Fabric E.

For the tabs, cut three 4½" × 6½" (11.5 × 16.3 cm) rectangles from Fabric E.

For the banner back, cut one 21½" × 45½" (54.8 × 116.3 cm) rectangle from the fabric for the backing.

YOU WILL NEED

¼ yd. (0.25 m) **Fabric A,** for background.

¼ yd. (0.25 m) **Fabric B,** for letters.

¼ yd. (0.25 m) **Fabric C,** for sashing.

⅜ yd. (0.35 m) **Fabric D,** for inner border.

⅝ yd. (0.6 m) **Fabric E,** for outer border and tabs.

1⅜ yd. (1.3 m) **fabric,** for backing.

Scraps of fabric, for stained-glass squares.

Four 3-yd. (2.75 m) pkg. narrow double-fold bias tape.

Pressure-sensitive dry adhesive, such as Stick 'n Stitch™ adhesive by EZ International.

Tear-away stabilizer.

1" (2.5 cm) grid, such as cutting mat or graph paper.

Rod or dowel, up to 1" (2.5 cm) in diameter.

Noel banner can be made vertically or horizontally. Instructions for the vertical banner, opposite, are included on pages 51 to 55. The horizontal banner above is made by changing the position of the letters and spacing five tabs evenly along the upper edges.

Diagram for the Noel Banner Letters

Scale. One square on the grid is equal to one square inch (2.5 sq. cm).

How to Sew a Noel Banner

1) Place a sheet of tracing paper over a 1" (2.5 cm) grid, such as a cutting mat. Make the full-size letters, using the diagram (left); enlarge letters, using grid lines as a guide.

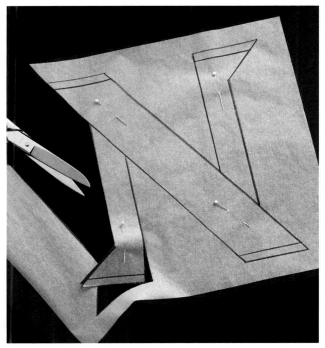

2) Add ¼" (6 mm) seam allowances to upper and lower edges of letters. Cut the letters from fabric.

3) Apply pressure-sensitive dry adhesive to back of letters, following manufacturer's directions; position letters on background squares, matching raw edges.

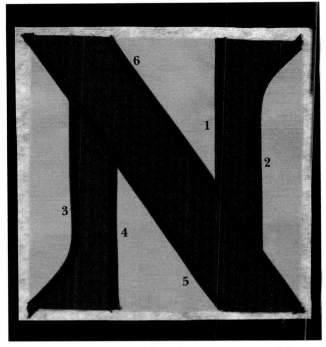

4) Trim off one fold of bias tape on narrower side to reduce bulk. With tear-away stabilizer under block, stitch bias tape over the raw edges of Letter N, along both edges of the tape, following sequence indicated. Curve bias tape around corners of Lines 2 and 3.

5) Stitch bias tape over the raw edges of Letter O as in step 4, following sequence indicated above. Curve bias tape around corners of Lines 5 and 6; extend the bias tape to edges of block on Lines 7 and 8.

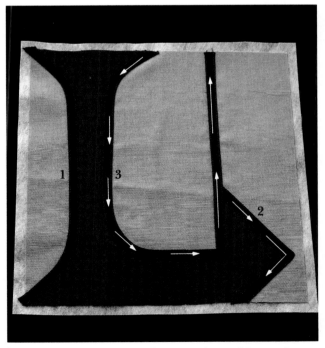

6) Stitch bias tape over the raw edges of Letter E as in step 4, following sequence indicated above. Use a continuous strip of bias tape for Line 2, and stitch in direction of arrows; miter square corners.

7) Stitch bias tape over the raw edges of Letter L as in step 4, following sequence indicated above. Miter square corners on Lines 2 and 3; extend the bias tape on Line 3 to edge of block. Remove tear-away stabilizer; press finished blocks.

(Continued on next page)

8) Pin short sashing strips to blocks, right sides together; stitch. Press the seams toward sashing strips. Pin long sashing strips to the blocks, right sides together; stitch. Press seams toward sashing strips.

9) Fold inner border strips in half lengthwise; finger-press. Apply pressure-sensitive dry adhesive to wrong side of stained-glass squares; position on inner border strips, so the opposite points of the squares are aligned along the fold.

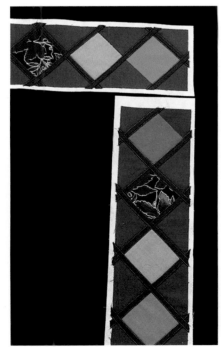

10) Pin bias tape over raw edges of squares, extending it into the seam allowances. With tear-away stabilizer under border strips, stitch close to both edges of bias tape. Set aside bias strips that will cross the inner border seams. Remove stabilizer.

11) Pin long inner border strips to sides of blocks, right sides together; stitch seams. Press seams toward blocks. Pin short inner border strips to the blocks, right sides together; stitch. Press seams toward blocks.

12) Pin bias tape over raw edges of remaining stained-glass squares where the inner border strips are seamed together. Stitch close to both edges of bias tape.

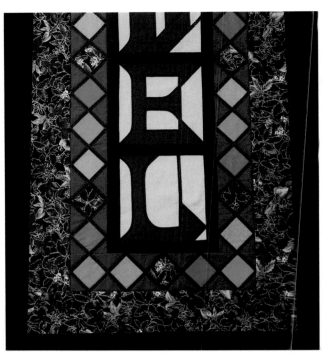

13) Pin long outer border strips to banner, right sides together; stitch. Press seams toward outer border. Pin short outer border strips to banner, right sides together; stitch. Press seams toward outer border.

14) Fold each tab strip in half, right sides together, to make 3¼" × 4½" (8.2 × 11.5 cm) rectangle. Stitch seam along edge opposite fold; press open. Turn right side out; press, centering seam.

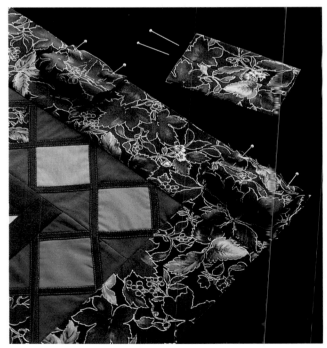

15) Fold tabs in half, with seams to inside, matching raw edges. Pin tabs to upper edge on the right side of banner, spacing them evenly and matching raw edges. Baste.

16) Pin banner front to banner back, right sides together. Stitch around all edges, leaving 6" (15 cm) opening. Turn banner right side out; press. Slipstitch opening closed.

Christmas Countdown Wall Hangings

Count down the days to Christmas with a Christmas tree wall hanging. Move one miniature ornament from the background to the tree each day beginning December 1 so the tree will be completely decorated by Christmas.

For body, the wall hanging is constructed with a layer of fleece or batting between the front and the back fabric layers. The Christmas tree is appliquéd to the front using a machine satin-stitch. Buttons, stitched to the tree and the background, serve two purposes; they hold the layers together, giving a quilted look, and also hold the ornaments in place.

Hang ornaments in the background area until they are ready to be used on the tree. Display the wall hanging from a rod or dowel, using the tabs across the top.

✂ Cutting Directions

Cut one 26" (66 cm) square each from muslin and fleece or batting.

Cut one 20½" (52.3 cm) square from the fabric for the background.

Cut two 2½" × 20½" (6.5 × 52.3 cm) rectangles from the border fabric, for the upper and lower borders; cut two 2½" × 24½" (6.5 × 62.3 cm) rectangles from the border fabric, for the sides.

Make the pattern for the tree as on page 53, step 1; cut one tree from fabric.

Cut one 2½" × 3" (6.5 × 7.5 cm) rectangle from the fabric for the trunk.

Cut one 24½" (62.3 cm) square from the backing fabric.

Cut four 2½" × 4½" (6.5 × 11.5 cm) rectangles from the border fabric, for the tabs.

YOU WILL NEED

⅔ yd. (0.63 m) fabric, for background.

⅓ yd. (0.32 m) fabric, for border.

½ yd. (0.5 m) fabric, for tree.

¾ yd. (0.7 m) muslin.

¾ yd. (0.7 m) fabric, for backing.

¾ yd. (0.7 m) fleece or batting.

Tear-away stabilizer.

Scrap of fabric for tree trunk.

Forty-eight buttons.

Twenty-four miniature tree ornaments, about 1" (2.5 cm) long.

One star ornament or button, for top of tree.

1" (2.5 cm) grid, such as cutting mat or graph paper.

Rod or dowel, up to ½" (1.3 cm) in diameter.

Diagram for the Tree

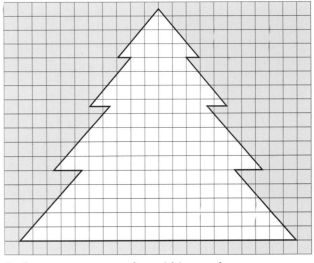

Scale: one square on the grid is equal to one square inch (2.5 sq. cm).

1) Place tracing paper over a 1" (2.5 cm) grid, such as a cutting mat. Make a full-size pattern for the tree, using diagram (page 57); enlarge tree, using grid lines as a guide. Cut the tree from fabric.

2) Center the 3" (7.5 cm) width of trunk on background fabric at lower edge; secure with glue stick. Appliqué sides of trunk to background as on pages 70 and 71.

3) Center tree on fabric, over trunk, 2¼" (6 cm) above lower edge; secure with pins or glue stick. Appliqué tree to background.

4) Place muslin square on the work surface; cover with fleece. Center the background fabric over fleece. Pin-baste layers together.

5) Pin around the tree through all layers. Stitch around outer edge of tree along satin stitching, to define outline of tree.

6) Pin the upper and lower border strips to background fabric, right sides together; stitch ¼" (6 mm) from edges through all layers. Turn borders right side up; pin to fleece and muslin layers.

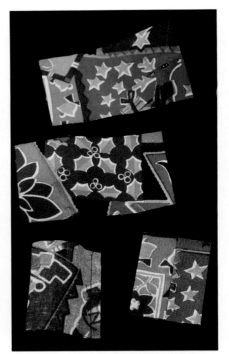

7) Repeat step 6 for the side border strips. Baste close to outer edges of border through all layers. Trim off excess batting and muslin.

8) Secure star ornament or button to top of tree. Stitch 24 buttons to background and 24 buttons to tree, spacing them evenly.

9) Fold one tab in half, right sides together; stitch ¼" (6 mm) seam along edge opposite fold. Turn tab right side out; press, centering the seam on back of tab. Repeat for remaining tabs.

10) Fold tabs in half, with seams to inside, matching raw edges; press. Pin tabs to upper edge on right side of wall hanging front, placing one tab ¼" (6 mm) from each side and spacing remaining tabs evenly across the top; baste.

11) Pin wall hanging front to backing fabric, right sides together. Stitch ¼" (6 mm) from raw edges, leaving 12" (30.5 cm) opening for turning; trim the corners. Turn the wall hanging right side out; press. Slipstitch opening closed.

Fabric Gingerbread Houses

Sew a delightful gingerbread house that can be used year after year. The possibilities for decorating the house are unlimited. Embellishments can include appliqués, buttons and beads, decorative machine stitches, and even outlining with fabric paints

The house is constructed in three sections. The side walls, end walls, and floor are stitched together to make the house section, and the roof and chimney are made as separate sections. The sections are made firm by inserting plastic canvas pieces into pockets on the inside. The plastic canvas pieces are easily removed so the house may be stored flat.

Make the gingerbread house from cotton broadcloths, calicoes, or Christmas prints. The fabrics can be backed with fusible interfacing if additional body is desired.

To create a winter scene, sew a few evergreens to display with the gingerbread house. The evergreens can be embellished with decorative machine stitches or with buttons or beads.

✂ Cutting Directions (for the gingerbread house)
From the fabric for the house, cut five 6½" × 10½" (16.3 × 27.8 cm) rectangles for the side walls, wall lining pieces, and floor.

From the fabric for the house, cut four 6½" × 9" (16.3 × 23 cm) rectangles for the end walls and end wall lining pieces.

From the roof fabric, cut one 10½" × 12½" (27.8 × 31.8 cm) rectangle for the roof and two 5½" × 12½" (14 × 31.8 cm) rectangles for the roof lining pieces.

From plastic canvas, cut six 6" × 10" (15 × 25.5 cm) rectangles; two pieces are used for each side wall and two pieces for the floor. Cut two 5" × 12" (12.5 × 30.5 cm) rectangles from plastic canvas for the roof.

Cut four end wall pieces from plastic canvas, two for each end wall, using the fabric end wall from page 62, step 1, as a pattern.

From the fabric for the chimney, cut eight 2½" × 3" (6.5 × 7.5 cm) rectangles for the chimney side pieces, end pieces, and lining pieces. From plastic canvas, cut four 2" × 2½" (5 × 6.5 cm) rectangles. The end pieces and the plastic canvas for the end pieces will be cut to shape on page 62, step 2.

From the fabric for the chimney, cut one 2½" (6.5 cm) square for the top of the chimney; from plastic canvas, cut one 2" (5 cm) square.

✂ Cutting Directions (for one evergreen)
Make the evergreen pattern using a tree-shaped cookie cutter as on page 16, step 1. From the fabric for the evergreen, cut two tree pieces, wrong sides together.

YOU WILL NEED

For the gingerbread house:
⅝ **yd. (0.6 m) fabric,** for house.
⅜ **yd. (0.35 m) fabric,** for roof.
Scraps of fabric, for chimney.
Three sheets of 13" × 22" (33 × 56 cm) plastic canvas.
Embellishments as desired.

For evergreens:
Scraps of fabric.
Polyester fiberfill.
Dowel, 1" (2.5 cm) in diameter; saw.
Acrylic paint, for tree trunk.
Embellishments as desired.
Hot glue gun and glue sticks.

How to Sew a Fabric Gingerbread House

1) Mark a point on end wall at center of one short side. Mark points on long sides 2⅝" (6.8 cm) from same short side. Draw lines connecting points, to form peak on end wall; cut on marked lines.

2) Center fabric for end wall of house over end pieces of chimney; trace peak. Trim ¼" (6 mm) from marked line, as shown. Repeat for lining of chimney end pieces. Trim two plastic canvas rectangles for chimney to match end pieces.

3) Cut and apply fusible interfacing to the pieces, if desired, following the manufacturer's directions. Embellish walls and roof with flat embellishments, such as appliqués (pages 70 and 71) or decorative machine stitches. Or embellish with fabric paints (pages 15 and 17); allow to dry.

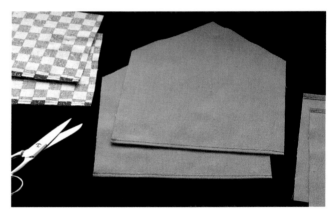
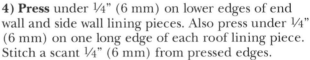

4) Press under ¼" (6 mm) on lower edges of end wall and side wall lining pieces. Also press under ¼" (6 mm) on one long edge of each roof lining piece. Stitch a scant ¼" (6 mm) from pressed edges.

5) Pin roof lining pieces to roof, right sides together, so pressed edges meet in center of roof. Stitch ¼" (6 mm) from all edges; press seams open. Turn to right side; press.

6) Insert one plastic canvas piece for roof into each pocket; trim plastic canvas slightly, if necessary.

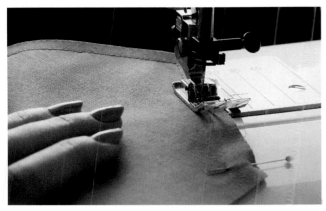

7) **Pin** end wall lining piece to end wall along peak, right sides together; stitch ¼" (6 mm) seam along the peak, leaving sides and lower edge unstitched. Press seam open. Turn to right side; press.

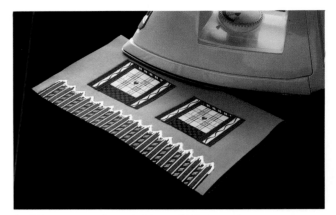

8) **Pin** upper edge of side wall lining piece to upper edge of the side wall, right sides together; stitch ¼" (6 mm) seam, leaving the sides and lower edges unstitched. Press seam open. Turn to right side; press.

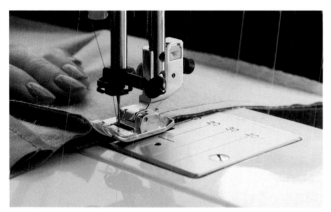

9) **Pin** side walls to floor, right sides together. Stitch ¼" (6 mm) seams, keeping lining pieces free; begin and end stitching ¼" (6 mm) from the ends. Repeat with end walls.

10) **Lay** gingerbread house flat, so floor is wrong side up. Glue-baste lining pieces to walls.

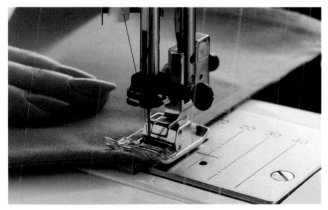

11) **Pin** side walls to end walls, right sides together. Stitch ¼" (6 mm) seams.

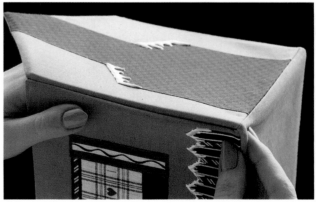

12) **Insert** two plastic canvas pieces into each pocket; trim plastic canvas slightly, if necessary. Turn to right side. Adjust plastic canvas to fit snugly into corners. Place remaining canvas pieces inside house on floor. Add additional embellishments, if desired.

(Continued on next page)

How to Sew a Fabric Gingerbread House (continued)

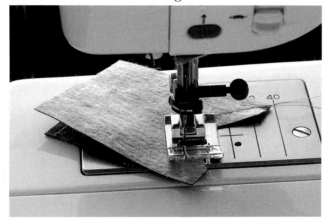

13) Finish the edges of chimney side and end pieces for lining as on page 62, step 4. Pin end piece to end piece lining around inside corner. Stitch ¼" (6 mm) seam, leaving sides and lower edges unstitched. Press seam open; clip corner. Turn to right side; press.

14) Stitch side pieces to side lining pieces as on page 63, step 8. Stitch top of chimney as for floor of house, steps 9 to 11. Insert one plastic canvas piece into each pocket and one into top of chimney. Position roof and chimney over house as desired.

How to Make an Evergreen

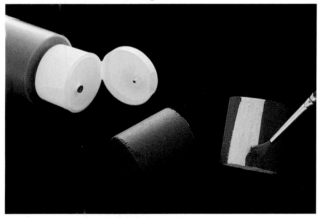

1) Cut 1" (2.5 cm) length from dowel for tree trunk, using saw. Paint trunk as desired with acrylic paint; allow to dry.

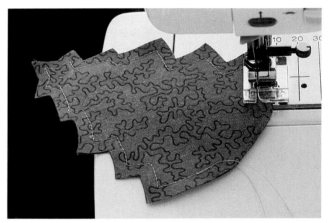

2) Trim away trunk area of tree. Stitch ¼" (6 mm) from outer edge of tree, using short stitch length; leave 1⅝" (4 cm) opening at lower edge to insert dowel for trunk.

3) Stuff the tree with polyester fiberfill. Trim seam allowance to ⅛" (3 mm). Secure trunk to tree, using hot glue.

4) Embellish tree as desired with buttons or beads.

Tips for Embellishing Gingerbread Houses

Checked, plaid, or striped fabrics can give the effect of shingles, bricks, or siding. Or rows of stitching can also be used to suggest bricks or shingles.

Wide rickrack, glued to the edges of the roof, can create roofline "icicles."

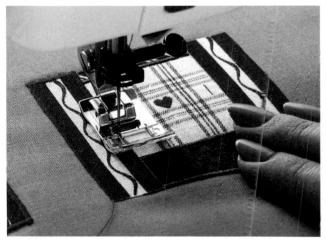

Contrasting fabric rectangles appliquéd to walls can be used to indicate windows and doors; add shutters to the windows for additional detail.

Cutout designs from printed Christmas fabrics can be fused to the walls of the house, using fusible web. Outline the designs with satin stitching, decorative machine stitching, or fabric paints in fine-tip tubes.

Buttons or beads can be stitched to the doors for doorknobs.

Miniature decorations, such as a wreath and bow, can be used to add dimensional effects to the house.

Appliquéd Aprons

Sew a holiday apron embellished with simple appliqués. The apron is designed to pull over the head and tie around the waist. It features a large, sturdy pocket divided into two convenient compartments.

Make the patterns for the appliqués by tracing around cookie cutters or by enlarging designs found on gift-wrapping paper. For more elaborate appliqués, you may use designs printed on fabric panels.

For durability, stitch the appliqué to the apron, using a machine satin stitch. When stitching, loosen the needle thread tension and use a machine embroidery thread that matches or is slightly darker than the appliqué. To prevent puckering, place a piece of tear-away stabilizer on the wrong side of the apron, under the appliqué, while stitching.

✂ Cutting Directions

Cut one 24" × 29" (61 × 73.5 cm) rectangle from the fabric for the apron. For the pocket, cut one 14" × 16" (35.5 × 40.5 cm) rectangle; for the binding, cut two 2½" × 53" (6.5 × 134.5 cm) bias strips.

YOU WILL NEED

⅞ yd. (0.8 m) fabric, for apron.

⅞ yd. (0.8 m) fabric, for pocket and binding.

Fabric scraps, for appliquéd designs.

Tear-away stabilizer.

Appliquéd designs for gingerbread men (opposite) were created by tracing around cookie cutters. The holly design (inset) was appliquéd to the pocket before the pocket was stitched to the apron.

How to Sew an Appliquéd Apron

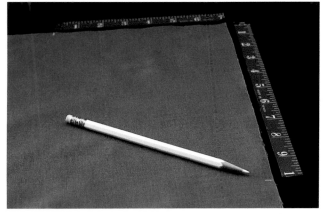

1) **Mark** point on rectangle for apron along one short edge, 7" (18 cm) from one corner; mark a point along long edge, 10" (25.5 cm) from same corner.

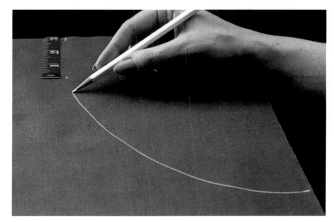

2) **Mark** a third point from same corner, measuring 3" (7.5 cm) from short edge and 7" (18 cm) from long edge. Draw a line, connecting the points with a slight curve, to mark armhole.

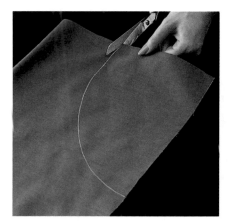

3) **Fold** the fabric rectangle in half lengthwise. Cut through both layers along marked line.

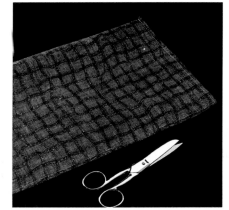

4) **Fold** rectangle for pocket in half, with right sides together, to make 8" × 14" (20.5 × 35.5 cm) rectangle. Stitch ½" (1.3 cm) seam on sides and bottom, leaving 3" (7.5 cm) opening; trim seams.

5) **Turn** pocket right side out; press. Pin pocket to apron, 9" (23 cm) from lower edge and 5½" (14 cm) from sides.

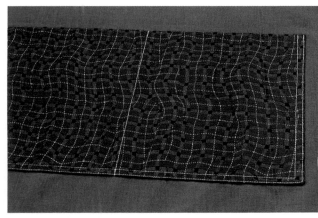

6) **Topstitch** pocket to apron close to pocket edges. Topstitch again ¼" (6 mm) from the first stitching. Stitch a vertical line through the center of pocket.

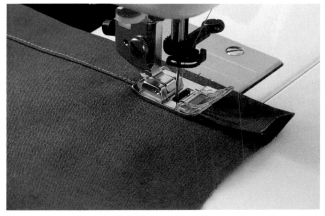

7) **Press** under 1⅛" (2.8 cm) on the upper edge of apron. Fold under ¼" (6 mm) on unfinished edge; press. Pin in place; stitch close to pressed edge.

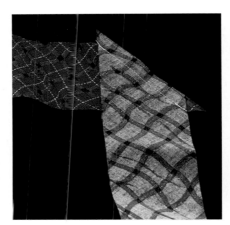

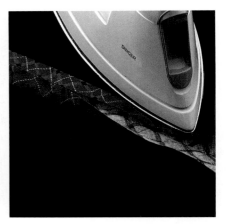

8) Narrow-hem the lower edge and sides of apron, using ⅝" (1.5 cm) seam allowance.

9) Join bias strips together in ¼" (6 mm) seam as shown. Press seam open; trim off points.

10) Fold binding in half lengthwise, wrong sides together; press. Open binding, and fold raw edges toward center; press.

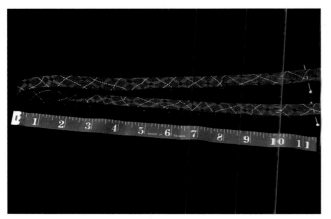

11) Fold binding in half crosswise; mark points 11½" (29.3 cm) from fold to mark distance for binding around neck.

12) Open binding. Pin right side of binding to armholes on wrong side of apron, raw edges even, matching markings on binding to upper edge of apron. Stitch along curved armholes, using crease in binding as a guide.

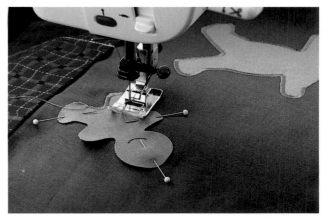

13) Fold under ½" (1.3 cm) on short ends of binding; press. Refold binding along lengthwise folds encasing raw edges; pin. Edgestitch binding to conceal seam and raw edges.

14) Cut the appliqué designs and stitch to the apron as on pages 70 and 71.

How to Sew a Satin-stitched Appliqué

1) Cut appliqué pieces as desired; do not add seam allowances. Mark any design lines, such as the mouth on a gingerbread man.

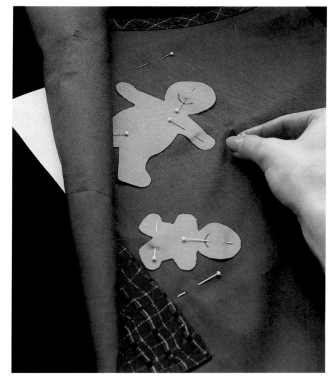

2) Position appliqués as desired, on the right side of the apron; pin or glue-baste in place. Place tear-away stabilizer on wrong side of apron.

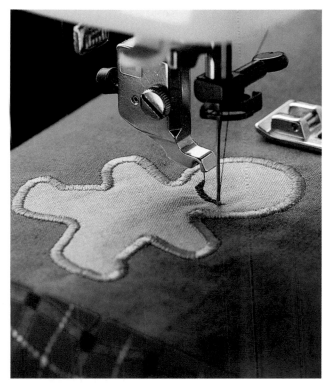

3) Set machine for short, wide zigzag stitch. Satin stitch around appliqué. Add details, using narrow zigzag stitch; taper stitching at ends. Remove tear-away stabilizer, taking care not to distort stitches. (Presser foot was removed to show detail.)

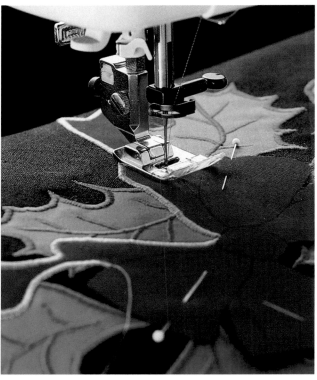

Layered appliqué. Apply and stitch first layer as in steps 1 to 3. Pin or glue-baste second layer in place; satin stitch and add details as in step 3. Repeat for any remaining layers.

Curves. Pivot the fabric frequently, pivoting with the needle down. For inside curves, pivot with needle at the inner edge of stitching **(a)**; for outside curves, pivot with needle on outer edge of stitching **(b)**.

Inside corners Stitch past corner a distance equal to width of stitch, stopping with the needle down at the inner edge of stitching. Pivot fabric, and satin stitch next side of the appliqué.

Outside corners. Stitch one stitch past edge of the appliqué, stopping with the needle down at outer edge of stitching. Pivot fabric, and satin stitch next side of appliqué.

Points. 1) Stitch, stopping when inner edge of satin stitching meets the opposite side of the appliqué. Pivot the fabric slightly; continue stitching, gradually narrowing stitch width to 0 and stopping at point. (Presser foot was removed to show detail.)

2) Pivot fabric, and stitch back over previous stitches, gradually widening the stitch width to original width. Pivot fabric slightly, and stitch next side of appliqué.

Tassels

Make a variety of tassels to use as decorating accents for the holidays. Tassels can be used to embellish wrapped packages, Christmas trees, stockings, or pillows. Make the tassels from either fringe trim or decorative threads.

For tassels from fringe, roll the fringe into a coil and decorate the upper edge with braid trim. Select from a wide variety of fringes in various thicknesses and lengths. For tassels from decorative threads, wrap the threads around an index card, and bind them together with additional lengths of thread. Small tassels can be made by wrapping fine threads around a 3" × 5" (7.5 × 12.5 cm) index card. Large tassels can be made by wrapping a larger quantity of thread or thicker thread around a large index card. Select

from cotton, rayon, silk, or metallic threads, combining different thread varieties to achieve interesting effects.

YOU WILL NEED

Fringe tassel:
7" to 9" (18 to 23 cm) fringe trim.
⅛ yd. (0.15 m) braid trim.
Hot glue gun and glue sticks.

Thread tassel:
Assorted decorative threads.
Index card or cardboard.
Decorative braid trim, optional.

Tassels from fringe hang from the tree branches above and decorate the pillow opposite.

Tassels from decorative threads are used in place of a bow to embellish a package.

How to Make a Tassel from Fringe

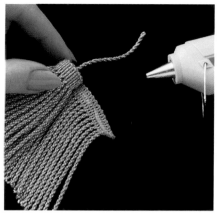

1) **Place** fringe wrong side up. Turn end cord of fringe over upper edge of fringe to make hanger for tassel.

2) **Apply** hot glue to wrong side of fringe along upper edge. Roll fringe tightly, starting from the end with the hanger, to make a coil.

3) **Wrap** braid around upper edge of fringe coil; allow ⅜" (1 cm) at each end of braid. Secure braid to the fringe coil with hot glue; turn under ends to conceal raw edges.

How to Make a Tassel from Decorative Threads

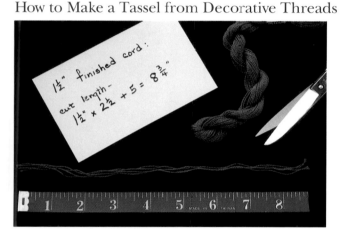

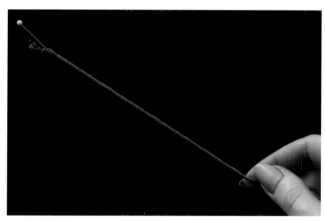

1) **Make** a twisted cord for hanger from decorative threads cut to 2½ times desired length of finished cord plus 5" (12.5 cm). Use number of strands equal to one-half desired cord diameter.

2) **Knot** ends of threads, and secure to a stationary surface. Twist strands of thread tightly, until the cord almost begins to crimp.

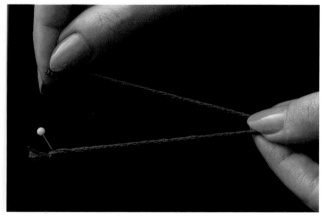

3) **Pinch** cord at center point. Bring ends together, holding them taut to keep the cord from untwisting.

4) **Pinch** ends together; allow sections to twist into a single cord. Knot end of cord at desired length plus about 1" (2.5 cm). Smooth cord to even out twists. Set aside cord until step 6.

5) Wrap decorative threads around index card until desired fullness is achieved. Clip threads at both ends of card; keep thread in a bundle with ends together.

6) Place cord from step 4 in center of thread bundle, with the knotted end extending about 1" (2.5 cm) beyond thread ends.

7) Bind bundle about ¼" (6 mm) from thread ends by wrapping tightly with length of thread.

8) Secure the end of binding thread by threading it through needle and taking a stitch through binding, as shown; trim end.

9) Fold the threads down around binding. Secure by binding tassel as in steps 7 and 8, about 1" (2.5 cm) from top. Knot in cord must be below the binding thread. Clip threads even at lower edge of tassel.

10) Pull on cord until knot in cord reaches binding thread. Push the top of tassel down to create a pouf. Hand-stitch braid trim around binding, if desired.

Wired Ribbons

Wired ribbon, or French ribbon, can be easily and inexpensively made, using a conventional sewing machine or a serger. Use wired ribbons to embellish items such as candlesticks, packages, garlands, and baskets. Make wired ribbon from fabrics that look attractive on both the right and wrong sides. Fabrics like organza, lamé, taffeta, brocade, and tapestry work well.

Beading wire, available at craft stores, is stitched to the edges of the ribbon to make the ribbon easy to manipulate and arrange. Choose a beading wire that will support the weight of the fabric. Beading wire is available in several gauges. The larger the gauge number, the finer the wire. Use a thin wire, such as a 32-gauge, for voile, organza, or other lightweight fabrics. Use a thicker wire, such as a 28-gauge, for heavier fabric, like tapestry.

Wired ribbon can be made using a zigzag stitch on a conventional sewing machine, or a rolled hem stitch or a 3-thread overlock stitch on a serger. When using the zigzag method, insert the wire into a pressed fold at the edge of the ribbon strip; the fold strengthens the edge. Use a pintuck foot to keep the wire at the fold while stitching. Excess fabric is trimmed after stitching.

A rolled hem stitch is an attractive edge finish on lightweight fabrics, but for heavier fabrics, a 3-thread overlock stitch is used. To achieve good thread coverage on rolled hems, use a short stitch length, and stitch with woolly nylon thread in the upper looper of the serger. For a 3-thread overlock stitch, use a short stitch length with a decorative thread in the upper looper. This stitch produces a wider edge finish than the other two stitches.

✂ Cutting Directions

Cut the fabric strips to the desired lengths and 1" (2.5 cm) wider than the desired finished width of the ribbon.

YOU WILL NEED

Fabric, such as organza, lamé, taffeta, brocade, or tapestry.
Beading wire, gauge depending on the fabric selected.

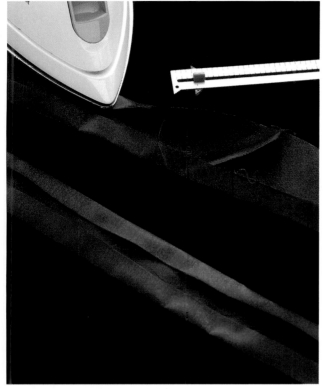

1) **Piece** fabric strips on the bias as necessary, stitching narrow seams. Press under ½" (1.3 cm) on long edges of fabric strip.

2) **Insert** beading wire into fold on the edge of fabric strip. Position folded edge of fabric strip under the presser foot; hold threads and wire firmly.

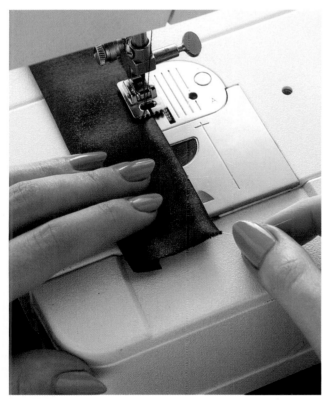

3) **Encase** wire by stitching over edge of fold, using narrow, closely spaced zigzag stitch. Repeat on the opposite side of the fabric strip.

4) **Trim** excess fabric from the underside of ribbon, using small, sharp scissors.

How to Make Wired Ribbon Using the Rolled Hem Stitch on a Serger

1) Piece fabric strips on the bias as necessary, stitching narrow seams. Adjust serger for rolled hem stitch. Stitch along strip for 2" (5 cm), trimming scant ½" (1.3 cm); stop, and lift presser foot. Place beading wire under back of foot, then over front; lower the presser foot.

2) Hold wire to the right of needle. Stitch over wire, trimming excess fabric; stitches roll to underside.

How to Make Wired Ribbon Using the 3-thread Overlock Stitch on a Serger

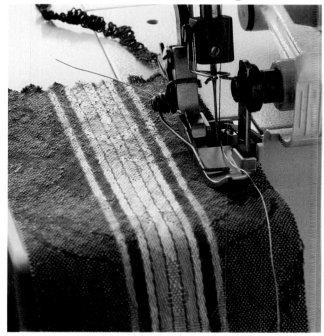

1) Piece fabric strips on the bias as necessary, stitching narrow seams. Adjust serger for balanced 3-thread stitch. Stitch along strip for 2" (5 cm), trimming a scant ½" (1.3 cm); stop, and lift presser foot. Place beading wire under back of foot, then over front; lower presser foot.

2) Hold wire to the right of needle. Stitch over wire, trimming excess fabric; threads lock together at the edge of fabric.

Fabric gift wraps (left to right) include circular gift wrap, rolled gift wrap, gift bag, and circular gift wrap. All styles are reversible.

Fabric Gift Wraps

Wrap packages creatively with fabric gift wraps. Choose from three styles, including circular gift wraps, rolled gift wraps, or gift bags. Make the gift wraps from lightweight to mediumweight fabrics, such as satin, taffeta, lamé, or seasonal broadcloth prints. Line the gift wraps with contrasting fabrics; the wraps can then be reversed and used with different trimmings for a new look the following year. Embellish the gift wraps with coordinating trims, such as wired ribbon (page 76)

or cording. Purchased end caps may be applied to the ends of the cording, if desired.

The circular gift wrap is ideal for baked goods and soft garment accessories, such as slippers, mittens, or socks. The rolled gift wrap works well for soft gift items, such as articles of clothing, that can be folded into rectangles. Custom-sized gift bags can be used for bottles and other items that are difficult to wrap.

✂ Cutting Directions

For the circular gift wrap, cut one circle each from outer fabric and lining as on page 82, steps 1 and 2.

For the rolled gift wrap, cut one rectangle each from outer fabric and lining, 4" (10 cm) larger than gift on all sides.

For the gift bag, cut two rectangles each from outer fabric and lining, using the method on page 83, step 1, to determine the size of the rectangles.

YOU WILL NEED

Fabrics, for gift wrap and contrasting lining.

Rubber band.

Ribbon or cording.

End caps, for cording, optional.

How to Sew a Circular Gift Wrap

1) **Position** the gift as it will be placed in center of gift wrap. Determine diameter of the circle by measuring around the gift as shown and adding 4" to 10" (10 to 25 cm) for heading and seam allowances.

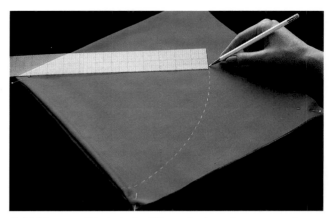

2) **Fold** outer fabric in half lengthwise, then crosswise. Using a straightedge and pencil, mark an arc on the fabric, measuring one-half the desired diameter of circle from folded center of fabric. Cut on marked line through all layers; mark raw edge at foldlines. Cut lining to same size; mark.

3) **Pin** the outer fabric to lining, right sides together, matching marks; stitch ¼" (6 mm) from raw edges, leaving 4" (10 cm) opening for turning.

4) **Turn** right side out; press. Slipstitch opening closed. Center the gift on the fabric. Draw fabric around gift, securing it with rubber band. Adjust folds; tie ribbon or cording around top, concealing rubber band.

How to Sew a Rolled Gift Wrap

1) **Pin** outer fabric to lining, right sides together; stitch ¼" (6 mm) from raw edges, leaving 4" (10 cm) opening for turning.

2) **Turn** the rectangle right side out; press. Slipstitch the opening closed. Center gift on fabric, allowing space around all sides. Roll up rectangle.

3) **Draw** up fabric at ends, securing it with rubber bands. Adjust folds; tie cording or ribbon around ends, concealing rubber band.

How to Sew a Gift Bag

1) **Measure** height, width, and depth of gift as it will be inserted in gift bag; record these measurements. Determine size of rectangles for gift bag, with length equal to height and depth of gift plus desired heading plus 1" (2.5 cm); width of rectangle is equal to width and depth of gift plus 1" (2.5 cm).

2) **Cut** rectangles from the outer fabric and lining as determined in step 1. Pin the rectangles right sides together; stitch ¼" (6 mm) from raw edges, leaving top of gift bag open. Repeat for the lining, leaving 3" (7.5 cm) opening on one side near top.

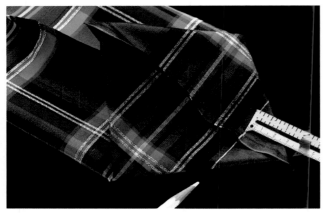

3) **Fold** gift bag at bottom so side seam is aligned to bottom seam; pin. Measure from the corner across seams a distance equal to one-half the depth of the gift; mark point on seamline. Draw a line through point, perpendicular to seamline.

4) **Stitch** along marked line; trim close to stitching. Repeat steps 3 and 4 for opposite corner, and repeat for corners of lining.

5) **Place** outer bag inside lining, right sides together. Pin upper edges, raw edges even; stitch ¼" (6 mm) from edge. Turn right side out through opening in lining. Hand-stitch opening closed.

6) **Insert** lining; lightly press upper edge. Insert gift into bag; draw fabric up around gift, securing it with a rubber band. Tie ribbon or cording around top, concealing rubber band.

Easter

Old-fashioned Easter Rabbits

Sew a nostalgic Easter rabbit with cut-on arms and legs. The simple pattern can be easily made, using the partial pattern pieces on page 89. The hand-embroidered facial details and covered-button tail add to the old-fashioned quality of the rabbit. For durability, choose a textured wool, wool flannel, decorator cotton, or corduroy. For a dressier look, select fabrics such as velveteen or brocade. Tie a contrasting ribbon bow around the neck of the rabbit for an additional embellishment.

Embroider the nose, mouth, whiskers, and outer two lines marked for the eyes, using an outlining stitch, and fill in the centers of the eyes, using a satin stitch. Three strands of embroidery floss are used for both embroidery stitches.

✂ Cutting Directions

Trace the partial pattern pieces (page 89) and make the full-size rabbit pattern as in step 1, below. Cut the front and back pieces from fabric, placing the center dotted line on the fold.

YOU WILL NEED

5/8 yd. (0.6 m) fabric, such as velveteen, brocade, chintz, wool, or corduroy.

Embroidery floss, for embroidered facial details.

Polyester fiberfill.

Button kit, for 1⅛" (2.8 cm) button, to be covered for tail.

Pinking shears, optional.

How to Sew an Old-fashioned Easter Rabbit

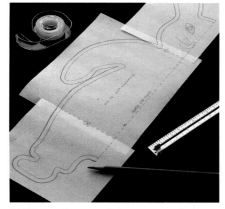

1) Trace the partial pattern pieces (page 89) onto tracing paper. Make full-size pattern by taping pieces A, B, and C together, matching notches and dotted lines. Add ¼" (6 mm) seam allowances.

2) Cut front and back pieces from fabric, above. Transfer the pattern markings for eyes, nose, mouth, and whiskers onto the right side of rabbit front. Transfer placement mark for tail onto rabbit back. Embroider facial details as on page 88.

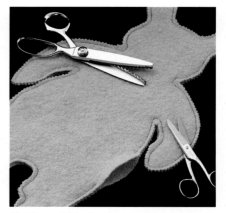

3) Pin rabbit front to rabbit back, right sides together. Stitch around rabbit, leaving 3" (7.5 cm) opening on one side. Clip seam allowances along curves. Or notch outer curves using pinking shears, and clip the inner curves with scissors.

(Continued on next page)

How to Sew an Old-fashioned Easter Rabbit (continued)

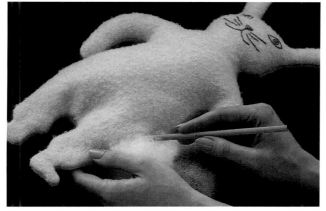

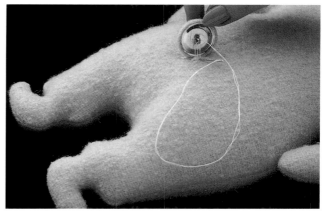

4) Turn rabbit right side out; stuff with polyester fiberfill until plump. Push fiberfill into ears, arms, and feet with the eraser end of a pencil. Hand-stitch opening closed.

5) Cover the button for tail with fabric, following the manufacturer's directions. Hand-stitch to back of rabbit at tail placement mark.

How to Embroider the Facial Details

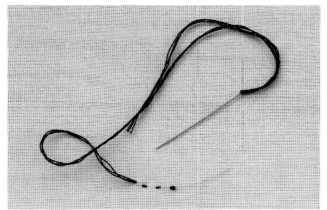

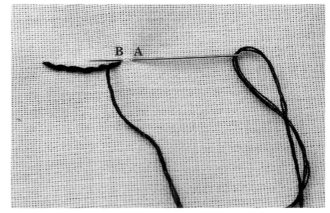

Outline stitch. 1) Secure threads by inserting needle along marked line about ½" (1.3 cm) to right of the starting point. Take short running stitches, as shown, until starting point is reached. Bring threaded needle through fabric from underside, at starting point.

2) Take backstitches by inserting needle to underside at Point A and up a scant ⅛" (3 mm) away at Point B. Continue stitching along marked line to end. Secure threads on underside of fabric.

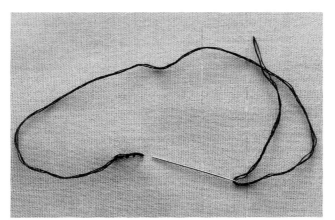

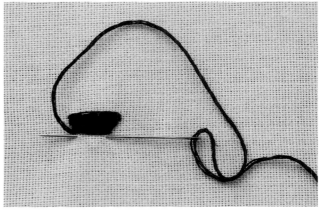

Satin stitch. 1) Secure the threads as in step 1, above. Bring needle through the fabric from underside on marked line. Insert needle on marked line directly opposite to make first stitch.

2) Fill in desired area with closely spaced parallel stitches. Secure threads on underside of fabric.

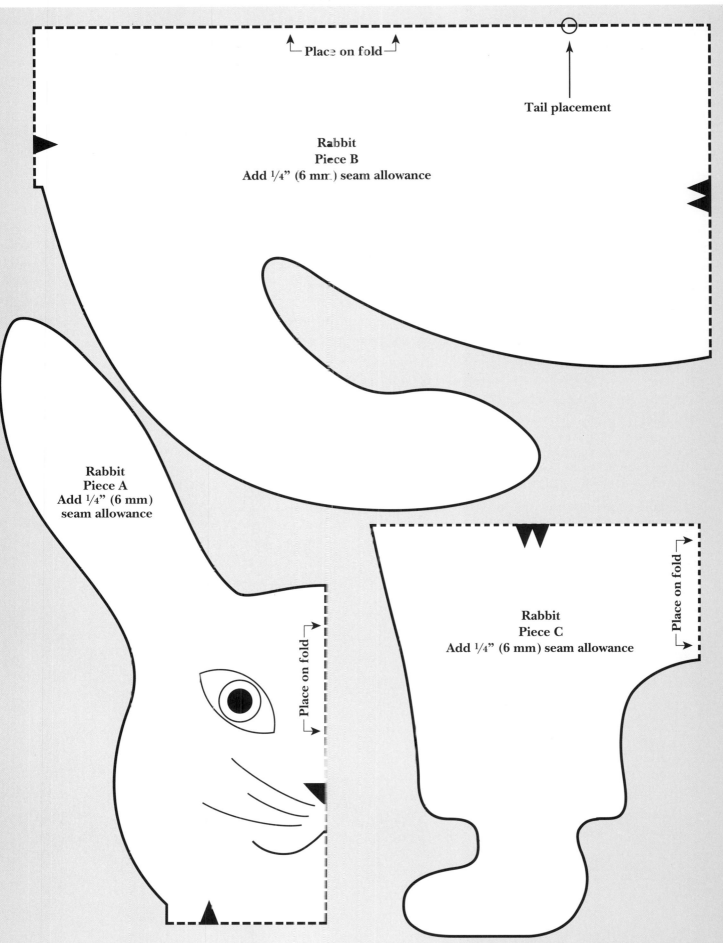

Place on fold

Tail placement

Rabbit
Piece B
Add ¼" (6 mm) seam allowance

Rabbit
Piece A
Add ¼" (6 mm)
seam allowance

Place on fold

Rabbit
Piece C
Add ¼" (6 mm) seam allowance

Place on fold

Easter Baskets

Decorate a wicker basket for Easter by covering it with bows of various sizes and colors. Or embellish an open-weave basket by weaving in ribbons and adding one large bow.

Use satin, organza, or velvet ribbon in various widths. Wired ribbons work well because they are easily shaped. Use purchased wired ribbon or make your own as on pages 76 to 79. Strips of tulle may be used instead of ribbon. Secure the bows and the ribbon to the baskets with wire or hot glue.

YOU WILL NEED

Bow-covered basket:
Basket.

Ribbon, such as satin, organza or velvet.

Hot glue gun and glue sticks or fine-gauge paddle floral wire and wire cutter.

Woven ribbon basket:
Open-weave basket.

Ribbon, such as satin, organza, or velvet.

Fine-gauge paddle floral wire and wire cutter.

How to Decorate an Easter Basket with Bows Using the Wire Method

1) **Tie** ribbon into bows; trim ends as desired. Insert wire through loop in center of bow on the back side. Twist ends of wire tightly to secure.

2) **Insert** ends of wire into basket from the outside, placing wire into different holes of basket.

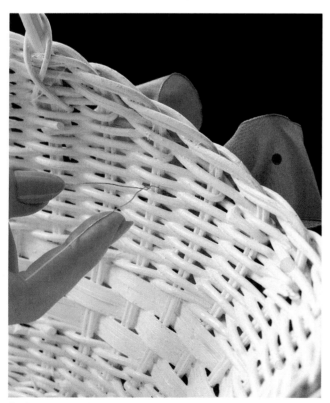

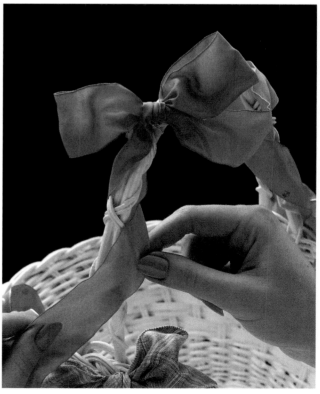

3) **Secure** ends of the wire by twisting them together on inside of basket. Trim excess wire; bend twisted ends downward.

4) **Tie** bow for handle; leave long ribbon tails. Secure bow to handle with wire; wrap tails around handle.

How to Decorate an Easter Basket with Bows Using the Glue Method

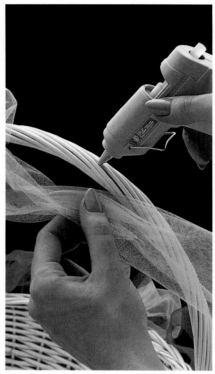

1) Tie ribbon into bows; trim ends as desired.

2) Secure bows to basket with hot glue; cover entire basket with bows, or concentrate bows in one area to create a focal point.

3) Tie bow for handle; leave long tails. Secure bow to handle with hot glue. Wrap tails around handle; secure with hot glue.

How to Decorate an Easter Basket with Woven Ribbon

1) Thread one or two ribbons into a large-eyed needle. Weave ribbons in and out of basket; to conceal starting and finishing points, overlap weaving at ends.

2) Tie bow for the handle and add wire as in step 1, opposite. Secure bow to handle, twisting ends of wire. Wrap tails around handle.

Lace-trimmed Table Linens

Dress up a table for Easter with a lace-trimmed tablecloth and napkins. Large tablecloths can be made with lace inserts to eliminate seams in the finished tablecloth. Fabric strips are pieced together, and lace is applied over the seams. Then, to create sheer inserts, the fabric is trimmed away under the lace. Consider the desired placement for the lace inserts when cutting the fabric strips and seaming them together. To finish the tablecloth, add lace edging around the outer edges instead of sewing a hem. To embellish napkins with lace, stitch a lace motif to a single corner of the napkin.

For the inserts and the edging, you may use a lace trim with two straight or two scalloped edges. Or for the edging, select a lace trim that has one straight and one scalloped edge. For embellishing napkins, a wide range of purchased appliqués is available, or motifs cut from lace yardage may be used as appliqués.

✂ Cutting Directions

Determine the desired finished size of the tablecloth, including the drop length, or overhang, on all sides; drop lengths may range from 10" to 15" (25.5 to 38 cm), including the width of the lace edging. When cutting the fabric strips for the tablecloth, remember to add one drop length for each side of the table and to take into account the width of the lace edging and the seam allowances. Because wide, scalloped edgings require matching, it is helpful to cut the fabric strips larger than necessary; any excess fabric will be trimmed from the outer edges after the edging is applied. Tips for positioning lace edging are given on page 96, step 1. Cut one 18" to 20" (46 to 51 cm) square from fabric for each napkin.

YOU WILL NEED

Fabric for tablecloth, amount determined by the size of the table.

1⅛ yd. (1.05 m) fabric, for four napkins.

Lace trims, for insert and edging of tablecloth.

Lace appliqués or motifs, for napkins.

How to Sew a Lace-trimmed Tablecloth

1) **Stitch** fabric widths, right sides together, in ½" (1.3 cm) seams; press. Pin lace inserts over seams, right sides up. Plan placement of lace edging by pinning it on fabric, right sides up, with edge of lace overlapping fabric at least ⅝" (1.5 cm); match lace motifs on sides and at corners. Pin out excess lace edging at corners; overlap and pin ends of lace.

2) **Remove** lace edging from fabric without disturbing the corners and overlapped ends. Fold the corner so inner edge forms 90° angle and outer edge is flat; pin.

3) **Clip** around motifs, so corner lies flat. Trim excess lace from wrong side, leaving at least ½" (1.3 cm) overlap. Pin in place.

4) **Stitch** overlapped layers of lace together, using short, narrow zigzag stitch; follow outline of design motif. Trim excess lace close to stitching.

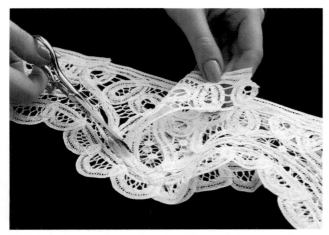

5) **Stitch** the overlapped ends of lace edging together, using short, narrow zigzag stitch; follow design motif in lace. Set aside lace edging.

6) **Stitch** lace inserts to fabric along both edges of lace, using short, narrow zigzag stitch.

96

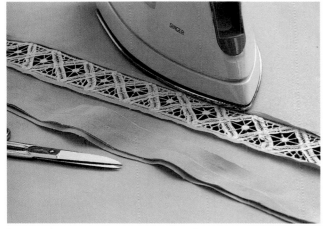

7) Trim fabric underneath lace ¼" (6 mm) from the stitching; press toward the fabric. Clip as necessary for scalloped lace.

8) Zigzag along both long edges of lace from right side. Trim fabric from wrong side, close to stitching.

9) Pin lace edging around outer edge of tablecloth, right sides up. Stitch along inner edge of lace, using short, narrow zigzag stitch.

10) Trim fabric from underneath lace, ¼" (6 mm) from stitching. Press toward fabric, clipping as necessary. Zigzag along inner edge of lace from right side. Trim fabric from wrong side, close to stitching.

How to Make Lace-trimmed Napkins

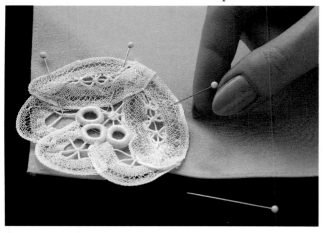

1) Narrow-hem napkin. Position the appliqué or lace motif on corner of napkin, right sides up; pin.

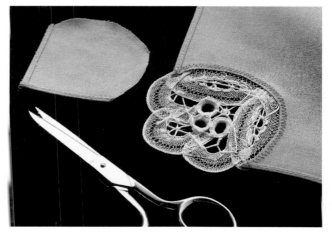

2) Stitch around the outer edge, using short, narrow zigzag stitch. Trim close to stitching.

Table ensemble features a lace-trimmed napkin (page 95) tied with wired ribbon (page 76). A lace doily basket (page 10) is used as a party favor. Braided ribbons were used to make the hanger for the basket.

Projects for Easter

Apron is decorated with appliquéd tulips. Use the instructions on pages 67 to 71 as a guide.

Cookie-cutter ornaments (page 15) hang from an Easter tree. Embellish the ornaments with fabric paints in fine-tip tubes.

Confetti placemats (page 103) are perfect for a child's party. The placemats are filled with plastic bunnies and eggs.

Halloween &
Thanksgiving

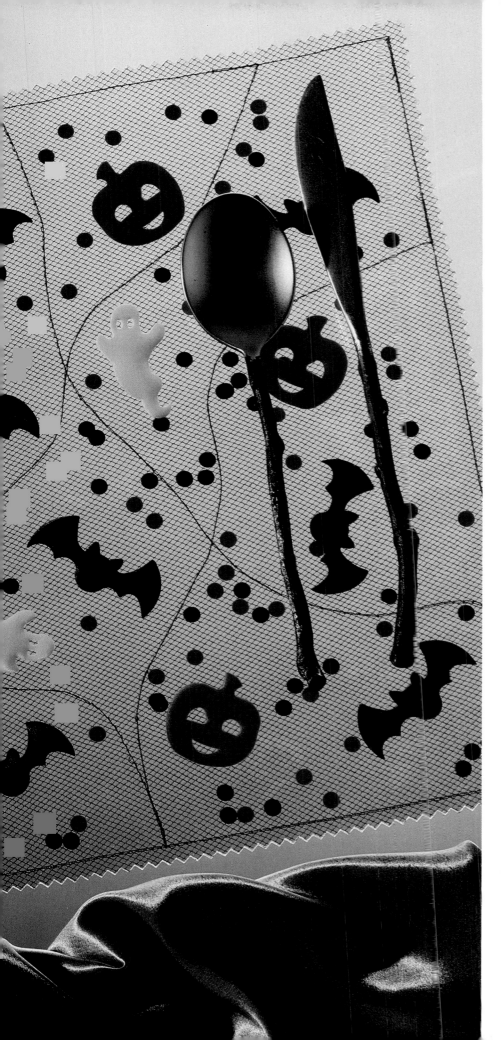

Confetti Placemats

Make durable confetti placemats for Halloween from two layers of clear vinyl, a layer of colored nylon net, and decorative holiday confetti. Small, flat Halloween decorations, like the jack o' lanterns, ghosts, and bats shown here, can be mixed with the confetti. Random rows of machine stitching divide the placemat into compartments.

For ease in stitching on vinyl, use a size 90/14 needle and a long stitch length. Loosen the needle thread tension, and stitch at a slow speed with a sheet of tissue paper under the placemat.

Look for seasonal plastic or metallic confetti in many shapes at craft and fabric stores as well as card and gift shops. The instructions that follow are for finished placemats that measure approximately 12" × 18" (30.5 × 46 cm).

✂ Cutting Directions

For each placemat, cut two 13½" × 19½" (34.3 × 49.8 cm) rectangles from vinyl and cut one 13" × 19" (33 × 48.5 cm) rectangle from net.

YOU WILL NEED

For four placemats:

1⅛ yd. (1.05 m) clear vinyl, 10-gauge or 12-gauge.

1⅛ yd. (1.05 m) of net, 36" (91.5 cm) wide.

Decorative metallic or plastic confetti or other small, flat decorations.

Pinking shears or scalloped scissors.

Spray adhesive.

How to Sew a Confetti Placemat

1) Mark a line on one piece of vinyl ¾" (2 cm) from each edge, using a permanent-ink marker.

2) Place the nylon net over a protected surface; apply spray adhesive lightly over net. Place confetti on net, at least 1" (2.5 cm) from edges; arrange as desired, pressing in place with finger.

3) Position the marked piece of vinyl over the net and confetti; smooth in place. Place vinyl and net over remaining vinyl piece; be sure any large air pockets are removed. Pin layers together outside marked line.

4) Stitch around placemat ¼" (6 mm) inside marked line; place tissue paper under placemat while stitching.

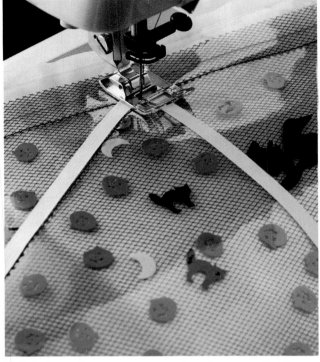

5) Stitch random rows across the placemat, dividing it into compartments; pivot fabric when possible for continuous stitching. Use tape as guide for stitching straight rows.

6) Remove tissue paper. Trim around all sides of the placemat inside marked lines, using pinking shears or scalloped scissors; cut through all layers.

Tips for Sewing Confetti Placemats

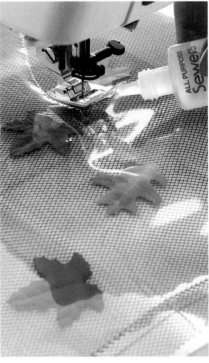

Cut plastic motifs from decorative wired garland, to mix with confetti when larger motifs are desired.

Use a monofilament nylon thread for stitching that is least visible.

Prevent presser foot from sticking to the vinyl by applying silicone lubricant frequently under front of presser foot.

Fabric Ghosts

Remnants of white fabric are used to create stiffened fabric ghosts. Quick and easy to make, these ghosts require little sewing and can be made in different sizes.

Plastic or glass beverage bottles are used to create a frame for supporting the fabric during assembly. A large ghost, about 16" (40.5 cm) tall, can be made using a 64-oz. (2 L) bottle and a balloon or Styrofoam® ball for the head. A smaller ghost can be made using a 16-oz. (0.5 L) bottle and a small Styrofoam ball.

For the best results, use lightweight to mediumweight fabrics of natural fibers, such as bleached cotton muslin, handkerchief linens, and cotton or cotton-blend batistes. The amount of fabric stiffener necessary to saturate the fabric varies with the weight and size of the fabric; ½ cup (125 mL) is enough for sheer fabrics and small pieces. Heavy fabrics and large pieces may require up to 1 cup (250 mL) of stiffener.

✂ Cutting Directions

Cut fabric square as on page 108, step 3. Cut two ½" (1.3 cm) fabric circles for eyes.

YOU WILL NEED

White fabric, such as bleached muslin, handkerchief linen, cotton and cotton-blend batiste.

Scrap of fabric, such as broadcloth, for eyes.

Fabric stiffener.

Aluminum foil, plastic wrap, masking tape, and cording.

Sheet of plastic, to cover work area.

Beverage bottle, 64-oz. (2 L), for large ghost; 16-oz. (0.5 L) bottle, for small ghost.

Balloon or 5" (12.5 cm) Styrofoam ball, for head of large ghost; balloon or 3" (7.5 cm) Styrofoam ball, for head of small ghost.

Embellishments, such as plastic or rubber spider or mouse.

Thick white craft glue, for securing embellishments.

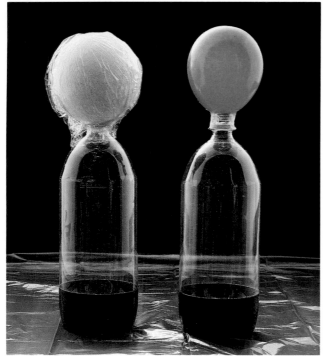

1) **Cover** the work area with a sheet of plastic. Press Styrofoam® ball firmly over the top of bottle; cover loosely with plastic wrap (left). Or, blow up balloon to measure about 5" (12.5 cm) in diameter; secure to neck of bottle with masking tape (right).

2) **Form** arms by cutting a length of aluminum foil twice the desired arm length plus about 6" (15 cm); crumple strip lengthwise, and wrap center of strip around neck of bottle. Cover foil with plastic wrap.

3) **Measure** frame for ghost, using a tape measure, from base in front, over the top, to base at back of frame; add to this measurement 2" to 4" (5 to 10 cm), depending on desired amount of fabric puddle. Cut a square from fabric to this measurement.

4) **Narrow-hem** fabric square, if desired. Drape fabric over frame, and mark placement for eyes. Cut eyes from fabric as on page 106. Appliqué eyes over the markings as on pages 70 and 71.

5) Pour fabric stiffener into bowl; dilute with water to a creamy consistency. Immerse fabric in stiffener; work stiffener into the fabric, making sure it is saturated. Remove fabric, squeezing out excess stiffener.

6) Drape the fabric, centering it over top of frame. Arrange the fabric in folds over arms. Using string, loosely tie fabric under head.

7) Press edges of fabric together at sides. Arrange fabric puddle, creating soft folds. Allow fabric and glue to dry completely.

8) Remove the bottle, plastic wrap, and foil, leaving Styrofoam head in place; if using balloon, pop and remove balloon. Attach embellishments as desired, using glue.

Stuffed Pumpkins

Stuffed fabric pumpkins are fun Halloween decorations, or they may be grouped for an autumn centerpiece, with a few artificial leaves or vines. Make them in two sizes, to be displayed together or with the scarecrow on page 114.

Each pumpkin is made from eight pieces. The leaves are created by making clips along folded strips of fabric. The strips are given a frayed appearance by wetting them, then machine drying. Select lightweight cotton fabrics, such as broadcloth, for the pumpkin and leaves. Use a cutting from a branch as the stem.

✂ Cutting Directions

For a small pumpkin, cut eight pumpkin pieces as on page 112, steps 3 and 4; cut two 4" × 7" (10 × 18 cm) rectangles for the leaves.

For a large pumpkin, cut eight pumpkin pieces as on page 112, steps 3 and 4; cut two 7" × 10" (18 × 25.5 cm) rectangles for the leaves.

YOU WILL NEED

⅓ **yd. (0.32 m) lightweight fabric,** for small pumpkin or ½ yd. (0.5 m) fabric, for large pumpkin.

⅛ **yd. (0.15 m) fabric,** for leaves on small pumpkin or ¼ yd. (0.25 m) lightweight fabric, for leaves on large pumpkin.

Cutting from a branch, for stem.

Hot glue gun and glue sticks.

How to Sew a Stuffed Pumpkin

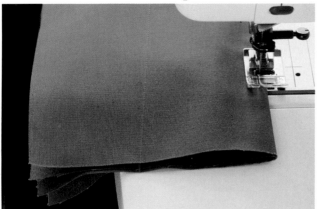

1) Cut rectangles for leaves from fabric as on page 111. Place rectangles for leaves wrong sides together, and fold in half crosswise. Edgestitch next to fold through all layers.

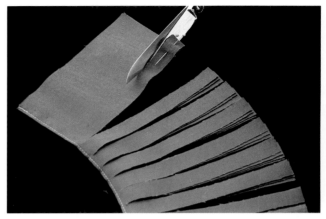

2) Make fringed leaves by clipping the fabric at ½" (1.3 cm) intervals, along edges opposite fold; clip to, but not through, stitching. Wet clipped fabric and squeeze out excess water; dry in machine dryer with towels, to fray edges of leaves.

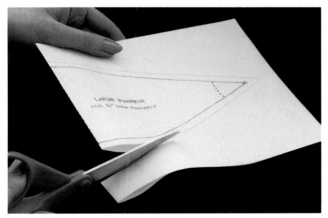

3) Trace partial pattern, opposite, onto tracing paper; add ¼" (6 mm) seam allowances. Fold paper on dotted line; cut on solid lines. Open full-size pattern.

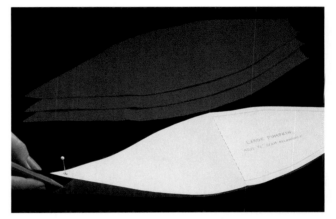

4) Mark dot on one end of the full-size pattern and dotted, curved line on the opposite end. Trim off the end of pattern on curved line. Cut pumpkin pieces; transfer dot to each piece.

5) Stitch two pumpkin pieces right sides together along one side, from curved end to dot, using 8 to 10 stitches per inch (2.5 cm); leave thread tails at curved end. Stitch remaining pumpkin pieces together, two at a time, to make four sections.

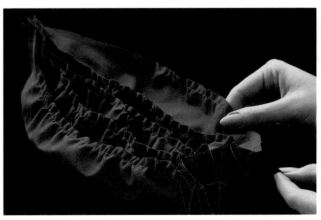

6) Stitch two pumpkin sections together, from curved end to dot. Continue to stitch remaining sections together until pumpkin is completed. Draw up thread tails to gather slightly along seamlines. Secure the thread tails.

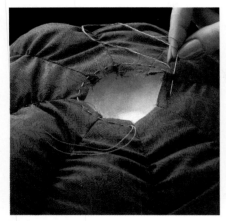
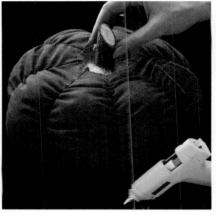

7) Stuff the pumpkin lightly with polyester fiberfill. Thread needle with buttonhole twist, and stitch around top opening, using running stitches; leave thread tails.

8) Insert cutting from branch into hole at top of pumpkin for stem; secure with hot glue. Pull on thread tails to gather fabric around stem; knot the threads.

9) Apply hot glue to stitched edge of fringed fabric for leaves; wrap strip around top of pumpkin.

Patterns for Stuffed Pumpkins

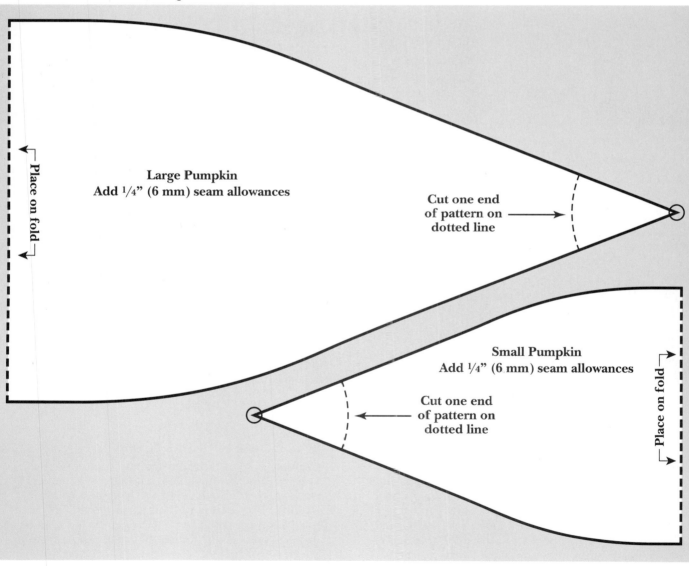

Place on fold

Large Pumpkin
Add ¼" (6 mm) seam allowances

Cut one end
of pattern on →
dotted line

Small Pumpkin
Add ¼" (6 mm) seam allowances

Place on fold

Cut one end
← of pattern on
dotted line

Country Scarecrows

This country scarecrow can cheerfully decorate a
buffet or mantel for autumn. Created from a block
of wood, a Styrofoam® ball, and four clothespins, the
scarecrow has a burlap face. The lightly padded
gloves and shoes are stitched so the raw edges are
left exposed for a ragged look. Dress the scarecrow
in a cotton shirt and denim pants. Make the pants

from an old pair of jeans, and add patches over the
knees. To create the look of straw around the neck,
wrists, and ankles, make fringe from cotton fabric
and fray it by wetting it, then machine drying it with
towels. You may also fray the edges of the hat brim by
wetting and machine drying the hat after the stitching
has been completed.

✂ Cutting Directions

For the head, cut one 15" (38 cm) fabric square from burlap. For the nose, cut one small fabric triangle. For the pants, cut two 10" (25.5 cm) fabric squares; if old jeans are used, center the squares over the side seams of the jeans. For the shirt, cut two 10" (25.5 cm) fabric squares for the front and back and cut one 8" × 20" (20.5 × 51 cm) fabric rectangle for the sleeves. For the fringe at the wrists and ankles, cut one 6" × 16" (15 cm × 40.5 cm) fabric rectangle; for the neck fringe, cut one 9" (23 cm) fabric square. Trace the patterns on page 119 onto tracing paper; cut four shoe pieces, four glove pieces, two hat crown pieces, and one hat brim.

YOU WILL NEED

Old jeans or scraps of denim, for pants.

Scraps of fabric, for shirt.

½ yd. (0.5 m) burlap, for head.

¼ yd. (0.25 m) cotton fabric, for fringe.

Block of wood, 2" × 4" × 6" (5 × 10 × 15 cm).

Four clothespins.

3" (7.5 cm) Styrofoam® ball.

2 yd (1.85 m) twine.

2½ yd. (2.3 m) cording or additional twine.

Scraps of firm fabric, such as felt or denim, for hat.

Scraps of fabric, for nose, shoes, gloves, and patches.

Buttons with four holes, for eyes; embroidery floss, for mouth; feather, for hat.

Rubber band; white craft glue; staple gun and staples.

How to Sew a Country Scarecrow

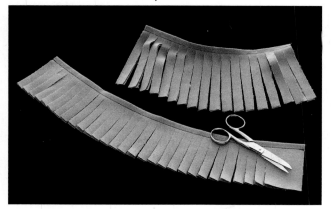

1) Fold fabric square for neck fringe in half crosswise; stitch ⅜" (1 cm) from folded edge. Repeat for fringe at wrists and ankles. Complete fringe as on page 112, step 2.

2) Place Styrofoam ball in center of the burlap, and gather the fabric tightly around it; secure with the rubber band.

3) Secure head to top of short end of wooden block, using staple gun and staples. Position one corner of fabric over front of block, and one corner over back; position remaining corners across top of block to form shoulders.

4) Stitch an X through the center of buttons for the eyes. Glue eyes and nose to head as desired. Mark the placement for the mouth; embroider, using the outline stitch as on page 88, steps 1 and 2. Make vertical stitches across mouth as shown.

(Continued on next page)

How to Sew a Country Scarecrow (continued)

5) Narrow-hem short ends of rectangle for sleeves using ½" (1.3 cm) hem allowance. Fold rectangle in half lengthwise, matching the raw edges. Stitch ½" (1.3 cm) seam; press. Turn tube right side out.

6) Mark center of tube, and align to center back of head at top of wooden block. Secure tube on each side of block at shoulder area with staples to form sleeves of garment.

7) Cut scraps of fabric for patches on pants. Fold the rectangles for pants in half as shown. Plan placement of the patches in center of rectangles; pin in place through single layer.

8) Stitch the patches to rectangles for pants, using a straight stitch, decorative stitch, or zigzag stitch.

9) Turn up ½" (1.3 cm) along the lower edge of the rectangles for pants; topstitch close to edge. Topstitch ¼" (6 mm) from first stitching; raw edge will be on inside of garment.

10) Pin the fabric rectangles for shirt to upper edge of rectangles for pants, right sides together, to make the garment; stitch ½" (1.3 cm) seam. Press seam allowances toward shirt.

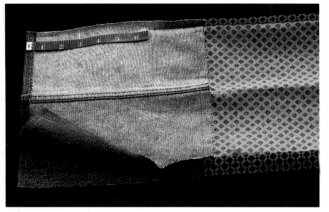

11) **Pin** garment rectangles, right sides together, on long edges; stitch ½" (1.3 cm) seam from top of shirt to 6½" (16.3 cm) from lower edge of pants. Press seams open. Seams become center front and center back of garment.

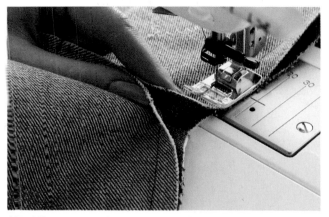

12) **Align** center front seam with center back seam. Pin the inner leg seams; stitch ½" (1.3 cm) seams, keeping crotch seam allowances free at center front and center back. Press seams open. Turn garment right side out.

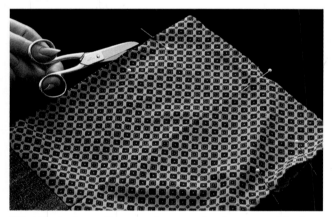

13) **Align** center front and center back seams. Mark points on each side of garment 2" (5 cm) and 4" (10 cm) from upper edge. For armholes, cut vertical slits on each side of garment between marks.

14) **Gather** garment ½" (1.3 cm) from upper edge with running stitches, using buttonhole twist. Insert wooden block into neck of garment; pull the sleeves through armholes. Draw fabric tight around neck, using buttonhole twist; knot threads, and trim ends.

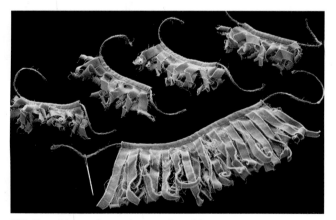

15) **Cut** fringe for wrists and ankles into four equal pieces. Insert cording or twine through the casings in fringe. Tie neck fringe around neck of scarecrow; knot, and trim ends.

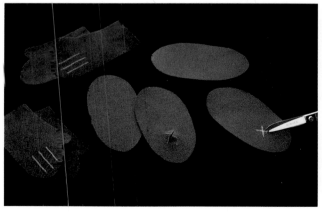

16) **Transfer** pattern markings onto two glove pieces and two shoe pieces. Make slit in two shoe pieces for top of shoe as indicated by the X on pattern.

(Continued on next page)

17) Pin two glove pieces wrong sides together. Stitch ¼" (6 mm) seam around the glove; leave the straight end open.

18) Insert small amount of polyester fiberfill to pad lightly. Stitch along marked lines for fingers. Trim seam allowances around glove to ⅛" (3 mm).

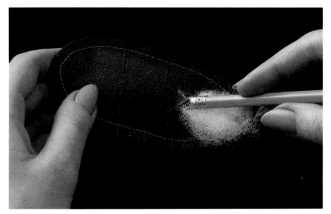

19) Pin top of shoe to bottom of shoe, wrong sides together; stitch ¼" (6 mm) seam around the shoe. Using eraser end of pencil, insert small amount of polyester fiberfill into X in shoe to pad lightly.

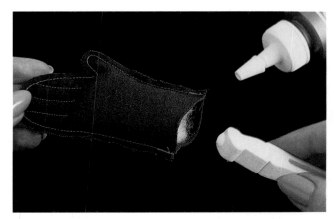

20) Apply glue to head of clothespin, and insert into glove. Repeat for the remaining glove and the shoes, inserting clothespin into X in top of shoe.

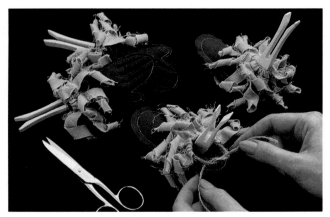

21) Tie the fringe pieces around each glove and shoe, using cording or twine; knot, and trim ends.

22) Apply glue to upper portion of fringe around one glove. Insert clothespin into sleeve; secure the sleeve around clothespin with twine. Repeat for remaining glove and the shoes. Tie length of twine around waist.

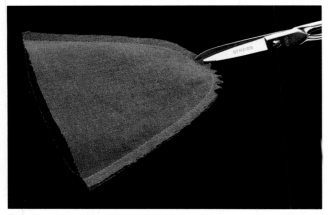

23) Pin crown pieces of hat right sides together; stitch ¼" (6 mm) seam around crown, leaving bottom open; notch curve, and turn right side out.

24) Stitch ends of brim, right sides together, in ¼" (6 mm) seam; edge-finish. Pin brim to the crown, matching seam to one crown seam; stitch ¼" (6 mm) seam. Glue hat to head. Glue feather to hat.

Patterns for a Country Scarecrow

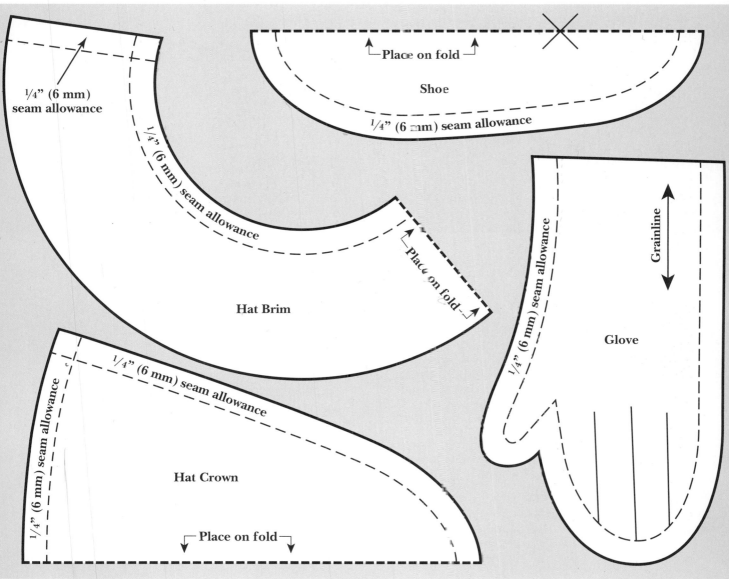

¼" (6 mm) seam allowance

↑ Place on fold ↑

Shoe

¼" (6 mm) seam allowance

¼" (6 mm) seam allowance

Place on fold

Hat Brim

Grainline

¼" (6 mm) seam allowance

Glove

¼" (6 mm) seam allowance

¼" (6 mm) seam allowance

Hat Crown

↓ Place on fold ↓

119

Fabric Cornucopias

Traditionally, cornucopias are filled with fruits or colorful squash, corn, and grains. Although often used as centerpieces for Thanksgiving, they may be displayed throughout the autumn season.

For a formal table setting, make a cornucopia from an elegant fabric such as brocade, tapestry, or moiré. To further enhance the look, embellish the opening of the cornucopia with decorative trims.

For a country harvest version, select a patterned or textured fabric that resembles the more common, basket-style cornucopias. A variation of this fabric cornucopia, made from a recycled quilt, is shown on page 125.

✂ Cutting Directions

Trace the partial pattern pieces (pages 122 and 123) and make the full-size cornucopia pattern as in step 1, opposite. Cut two cornucopia pieces from outer fabric and two from lining. Also cut two pieces from fleece.

YOU WILL NEED

⅝ **yd. (0.6 m) face fabric,** such as brocade, tapestry, moiré, corduroy, or wool.

⅝ **yd. (0.6 m) lining fabric.**

⅝ **yd. (0.6 m) polyester fleece.**

Polyester fiberfill.

⅝ **yd. (0.6 m) ribbon,** cording, or trim, optional.

How to Sew a Fabric Cornucopia

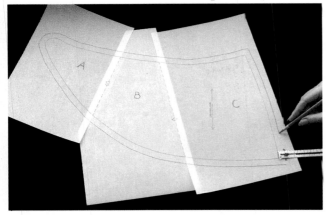

1) Trace partial pattern pieces (pages 122 and 123) onto tracing paper. Make full-size pattern by taping pieces A, B, and C together, matching notches and dotted lines; add ½" (1.3 cm) seam allowances.

2) Cut cornucopia pieces from outer fabric, lining, and fleece, opposite. Pin fleece to wrong sides of cornucopia pieces; baste.

3) Pin cornucopia pieces right sides together. Stitch ½" (1.3 cm) seam around cornucopia, leaving opening of cornucopia unstitched; stitch again next to first row of stitching, within seam allowances. Trim close to stitches. Turn cornucopia right side out; press lightly.

4) Pin the lining pieces right sides together. Stitch ½" (1.3 cm) seam around lining, leaving opening unstitched; also leave the bottom unstitched for 4" to 6" (10 to 15 cm). Stitch again next to the first row of stitching, within the seam allowances. Trim close to the stitches.

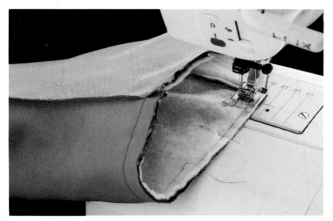

5) Place outer cornucopia inside lining, right sides together. Pin and stitch around the opening of the cornucopia. Turn right side out through lining. Stitch lining closed.

6) Insert lining into cornucopia; lightly press upper edge. Hand-stitch ribbon, cording, or trim around opening, if desired. Stuff the end of the cornucopia with polyester fiberfill to give it shape.

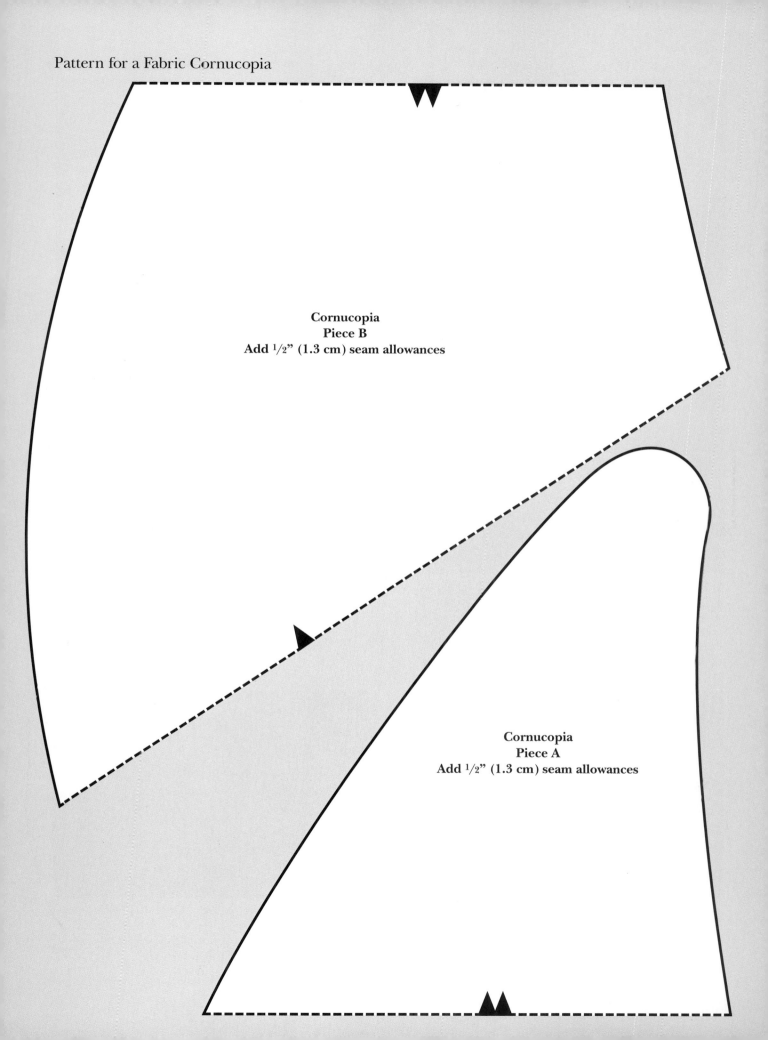

Pattern for a Fabric Cornucopia

Cornucopia
Piece B
Add $\frac{1}{2}$" (1.3 cm) seam allowances

Cornucopia
Piece A
Add $\frac{1}{2}$" (1.3 cm) seam allowances

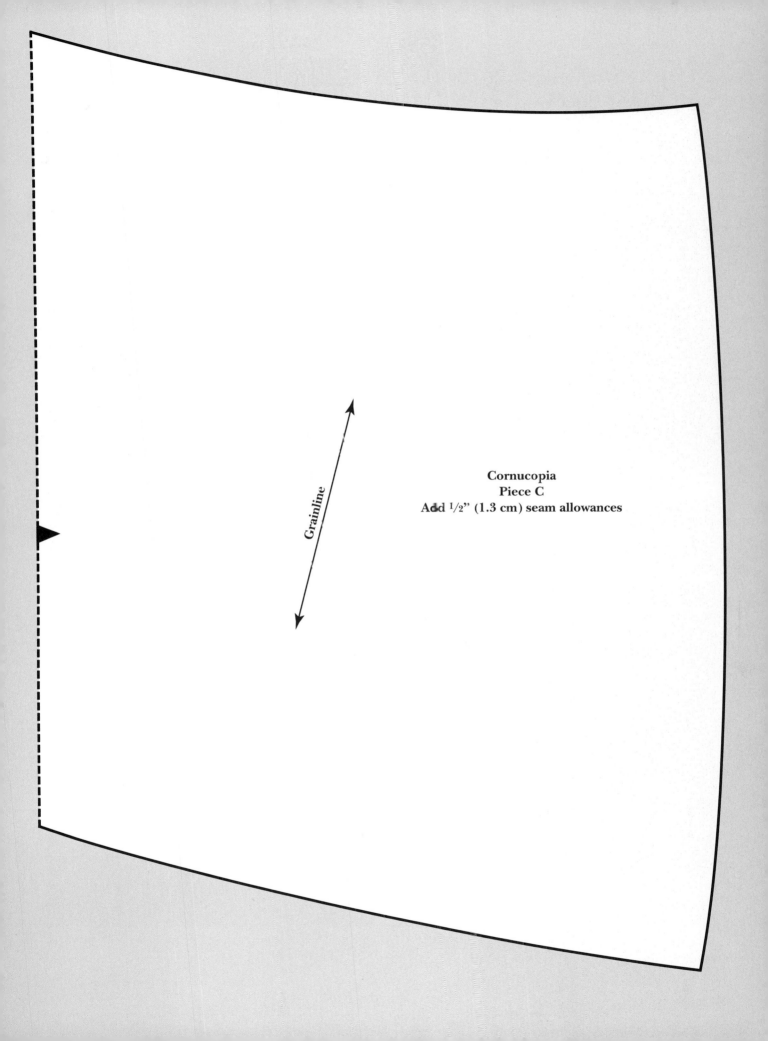

Cornucopia
Piece C
Add 1/2" (1.3 cm) seam allowances

Grainline

Projects for Halloween & Thanksgiving

Apron (page 67) is appliquéd with sunflowers. The apron can be worn throughout the autumn season.

Gift bag (page 80) is used for a hostess gift. Tie the bag with a coordinating wired ribbon (page 76).

Pair of table runners (page 43) decorate a table for Thanksgiving. The tapestry runners are embellished with gimp trim and tassels.

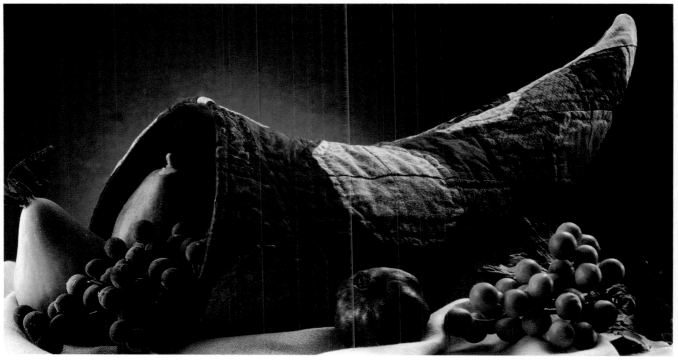

Cornucopia (page 120) is made from a recycled quilt.

Haunted house is a variation of the fabric gingerbread house on page 61. Cut designs from printed Halloween fabrics, and appliqué them to the sides of the house. Outline the designs with fabric paints in fine-tip tubes, and add dimension with purchased decorations.

Index

Cy DeCosse Incorporated offers
a variety of how-to books. For
information write:
  Cy DeCosse Subscriber Books
  5900 Green Oak Drive
  Minnetonka, MN 55343